MY DARLING OLGA

FOLKE
JONSSON
LETTERS
1909-1961

Copyright © Leif Södergren 2014

All rights reserved.
Apart from any use permitted by UK copyright law no
part of this publication may be reproduced, stored in a
retrieval system, or transmitted, in any form or
by any means without the prior written permission of the
publisher, nor be otherwise circulated in any form of binding
or cover other than in which it is published and without
a similar condition being imposed
on the subsequent purchaser.

Cover design by Leif Södergren

ISBN 978-91-979188-8-6

LEMONGULCHBOOKS
www.lemongulchbooks.com

For Donnie.
He knows why.

MY DARLING OLGA

FOLKE JONSSON LETTERS 1909-1961

EDITED BY
LEIF SÖDERGREN

CONTENTS

- 1   My Grandparents, Olga and Folke
- 4   1909 Engaged to be Married
- 7   Two Months Waiting and a General Strike
- 48   Almost Back to Work
- 65   Embroidery for Olga
- 92   1909 Olga in Paris. Certificates and Promises
- 109   1909 Finally Married!
- 111   1912 Oh, Not Pregnant Again
- 117   1913 Please Come Home Darling Olga!
- 154   1913 A New Apartment
- 180   1925 Folke at Lysholmen. Olga In Brussels
- 187   1926 Sickbed in Florida
- 195   1931 The Great Depression and a Sick Mother
- 203   Letters from Määtorp
- 215   1961 Folke's Last Letters
- 224   Olga and Folke
- 228   Family Facts
- 229   The Author

MY GRANDPARENTS, OLGA AND FOLKE

My American grandmother, Olga, met my Swedish grandfather, Folke, in Brussels in 1909. Olga was eighteen and Folke twenty-three. They met during the "Gilded Age", when the wealthy were extremely wealthy and the poor, extremely poor. In fact, much like today.

Olga and Folke who both came from well to do backgrounds, married only ten months after they had met. They settled in Gothenburg on the west coast of Sweden and by the time Olga was thirty-two, she had borne eight children.

Olga, being American, had her family in Florida and Folke soon came to realize that if you marry a woman from another continent, and this woman is charmingly independent, innovative and brave, and has her own means to boot, she is bound to want to visit her native country some time -- or several times -- or more than several times.

In those days, travelling to America from Sweden meant a long complicated journey and Olga was usually gone for several months each visit. It is said that absence makes the heart grow fonder, but to Folke, a sensitive soul, the long separations were quite painful and he could not wait for his darling Olga to return. He "talked" to her when she was gone in his frequent letters. Folke's letters were always dated, the pages perfectly numbered and in the finest handwriting -- a joy to read.

My grandmother Olga saved his letters, all in their original envelopes, in neat little bundles held together with different coloured ribbons. The older Olga, would frequently take the letters out of their respective envelope as she once had as a young woman, and once more she was able to enjoy her husband Folke's warmth and passion.

I had no idea that grandmother Olga had kept these letters until my mother died and I received them together with a great deal of other family correspondence.

All these letters revealed Folke as a very loving father and devoted husband. I particularly appreciated finding this out in this way since I never had a chance to know my grandfather well. He died before he reached his 75th birthday. Olga survived him by almost twenty years.

I am not surprised that Olga and Folke fell in love. They were both artistically inclined, had similar backgrounds, loving and generous parents and were themselves lovingly open-hearted. They were both keenly interested in other people and they both preferred to emphasize the positive in people or a situation and never sought out the negative.

They made a loving home for their children and their friends. Olga and Folke's friends and relatives all felt that Olga and Folke's home was somehow theirs also, wide open for them to visit whenever they wished to.

All this hospitality was possible because Olga and Folke had a cook and do-it-all, the superhuman "Linnea" who was enormously loyal and devoted to the two of them. By staying with them as long as they both lived, no doubt because they were interesting, good and loving people, she guaranteed in later days, that Folke and Olga could live a life-style that very few enjoyed. She would never have stayed with them had she not felt happy and "at home".

I am not surprised that Folke adored his wife. Olga had a very special charm and humour that made her the center of whatever situation she found herself. She was very secure within herself and made one feel very special and important.

It was always interesting and a pleasure to be around grandmother Olga. A day does not go by when I do not think of her. My mother felt the same about her mother.

Olga and Folke corresponded in English as Olga was American and preferred writing in English. Had my grandfather Folke married a Swedish woman who had stayed at home, there would not be this stack of his letters today. The letters that grandmother so wisely kept, are a testament to Folke's devotion to her. He never intended the letters to be shown to others, but more than one hundred years have passed since Folke wrote them to his darling Olga. I have enjoyed getting to know my grandfather in this way and I think others, not only relatives, should also share that privilege.

1909
ENGAGED TO BE MARRIED

When Olga and Folke met in 1909, they both lived in the same boarding house in Brussels. Olga and her American siblings had been brought to Europe by their parents to get a cultured "finish" as it was called then. My grandmother years later, in an interview, said that getting married was a welcome escape from school and travels all over Europe. When she met Folke, she had been away from her home town Jacksonville in Florida, for four years. Together with her mother and her father who came over for the summers, the family went on extensive trips from country to country.

The summers were hot and perhaps not the best time for teenagers to walk around in crowded cities and hot museums. In those days people did not wear T-shirts to stay cool, there were undergarments and more layers of clothing on top of those.

Olga fell wildly in love with Folke and he fell madly in love with her -- that was a welcome escape for Olga who could finally stop the incessant travelling and make her own home with Folke.

Marriage was arranged for October that same year. Olga was only eighteen which we might consider to be a very young age to marry, but she lived in the Edwardian era with roots in Victorian times when early marriages were encouraged, and:

"Once a young girl turned eighteen, her childhood was essentially over. The moment she put up her hair and lengthened her skirts, she was a woman. A coddled and protected woman, but a woman nonetheless. The putting up of the hair was the most important aspect of signifying one's status as a jeune fille à marier, or a young woman ready for marriage: no man bothered to address himself with other than the merest passing courtesy to a girl whose hair hung down her back. As soon as her hair was pinned up, everything changed, and for the remainder of the young lady's life, her hair would hang down over her shoulders only inside her bedroom or at a fancy dress ball." (Evangeline Holland-EdwardianPromenade.com)

Once Olga's parents had agreed to the wedding and the engagement was a fact, Olga and her family, her father William Dawson, her mother Anita Ball Dawson, her sister Una and her brother Willie, all went to Sweden to meet Folke's Swedish family. They spent most of the summer of 1909 at Särö, the exclusive seaside resort outside Gothenburg on the Swedish West coast.

The two families got along very well and Olga and Folke had the opportunity to be together during the summer. But they had to face being separated for two months until the wedding in Paris. Olga, her parents and her sister and brother, returned to the continent in early August to spend that time travelling through Denmark and Germany until the marriage in Paris took place.

During this time, Olga also was to assemble her "trousseau", the clothes, household linen, and other belongings collected by a bride for her marriage. She had been given a thousand dollars by her father for these expenses.

During this period, Folke would remain in Sweden working for his father's company Jonsson,

Sternhagen & Co. This meant that he would be without his beloved Olga for over two months and he wrote to her almost every day. The addresses on the envelopes were c/o Thomas Cook in Germany, Belgium and France. Two months separation is a long time for two people in love.

Little did Folke know that there would be many more separations during their long marriage, separations that would last much longer than those two months. But the future had not yet happened and this was 1909 and Folke was a young man in love, engaged to be married. Those two months seemed like an eternity to Folke especially since he could not do his usual work at the family business.

There was a devastating general strike and lockout in Sweden during all of August which had mill-owners such as Folke's father very concerned about the stoppage and loss of business but also concerned that their business could be hit by possible arson and sabotage.

TWO MONTHS WAITING AND
A GENERAL STRIKE

AUGUST 3, 1909
Having spent the summer in Sweden with Folke and his family, Olga and her family left for Copenhagen. Folke accompanied them to Malmö where Olga, her parents, Anita and William Dawson, her sister Una and brother Willy, had planned to take a boat across to Copenhagen where they would spend a few days and then go on into Germany. The separation was very difficult.

Folke, full of sadness, took the train back to Gothenburg, where he would spend all of August and September until he and his father set out for the wedding in Paris in early October. He wrote his first letter/card to Olga on his journey back to Gothenburg while he waited to change train at Åstorp.

The postcard was of the Royal Palace in Stockholm. It had been placed inside an envelope addressed to Hotel d'Angleterre in Copenhagen, Denmark

```
August 3, 1909
My Dearest, Dearest Olga,
Quite alone at the station at Åstorp. I feel I
want to say good night. The train will be here
in an hour. "Ledsen"(sad) to have my little
```

"älskling"(darling) so far away and knowing she will not be by my side for two long months. Dearie, I wish I could fly. You my Dear have your family but I, "your little baby", is quite alone. No flirting. I could never think of something like it when <u>you</u> älskling (darling) occupies my whole brain, heart and soul. Hope <u>you</u> don't flirt either.

    A long kiss my dear, my whole life. Think Dear, I can't get anything to eat as this little place has not even got a restaurant. I address this to the hotel in Copenhagen, but the next letter will be to Cooks.

    Give your Dear father and mother my best regards and Una and Willie -- must ring off. I kiss you a 1000000000 times in my thoughts because you can't get tired of that.

    I am always your loving, ever your baby
Folke

AUGUST 4, 1909

Folke is back in Gothenburg and ready to work. But Gothenburg and the rest of Sweden, was uncannily quiet, no work going on anywhere except in hospitals. There was a general strike, the biggest strike ever in the history of Sweden

A recession had caused many companies to lower the wages of their workers. When the workers did not agree, 80,000 workers in selected industries were let go (locked out) by their employers. The unions, not nearly as strong as they became later, responded with a general strike and Folke's father's mill and other business lay idle.

Businessmen feared unrest and sabotage and guards were posted for protection. Folke's father was no doubt glad to have his son around at this time.

Folke expressed his gratitude toward Olga's parents for allowing them to marry. Olga's mother who lived in Europe all year, must have seen the excellent qualities of Folke and had encouraged the marriage. Folke knows that they had Anita Dawson, Olga's mother, very much on their side from the very beginning when they met in early 1909. Four months later they were engaged and ten months later, they were married.

```
August 4, 1909
My own Dearest "lilla älskling"
(little darling)
```
Where is my Olga, where is she? Far away in another country but she is not far away from her little baby, is she? I feel she is with me.

Olga dear, hope you got my letter from the old station, but you must believe me I felt very sad going home that long tiresome way, but now I am in work again and have had a little rest and a lovely bath this morning.

Have not seen my father yet as he has stopped out at Särö today as nothing to attend to at the office as the mill is closed, no work down by the Quay and the workmen walking in the streets dressed up in their Sunday costumes. No fights whatever yet but perhaps they wait for the night.

Hope you liked hotel D'Angleterre and also the town. Hope you all arrived without any accidents. Have forwarded two postcards and two packets of newspapers that's all up to 1AM today.

Dear I wished I was in Copenhagen, how glorious but I am looking forward to October and then I hope time passes quick.

There's a kiss XXX my own Olga, Darling hope you take care of yourself. I suppose you wonder how many cigarettes have been in my mouth. Dear, sorry to say, one yesterday night, the third because, well no reason, of mischief I suppose.

I was thinking of you the whole time, but to

clear my thoughts I smoked. Today I have not yet smoked so I can probably reduce it to two today -- isn't he a good naughty boy, I mean I am not myself when I know you are so far away from me but you have my heart "tout a' fait".

Dear, write me now and tell me how long time you stopped in Copenhagen.

I've written today to your dear father just only to thank him for the time together -- I miss your father and mother very much Dear as I feel we have them quite on our side. Your mother, how kind to help us along with our hopes and your father giving his consent. I will not think how I should be, if things should have been otherwise.

Dear, give my very best regards to all. I wold give "mycket" (much) to take you in my arms and kiss you. I cannot write more, I nearly cry. Kisses in lots from your own always loving longing ever,
Yours Folke

August 5, 1909

Folke had received a postcard from Olga and was happy for the time being. He wanted her to write every day, at least a postcard. Folke was, and would continue through their life, to be the more diligent correspondent. With his excellent penmanship, his letters are a joy to read and easily accessible today. Olga's letters on the other hand, are very hard to read.

Folke missed Olga enormously, especially when he went out to Särö at his father's summer house 'Beau Rivage' where he and Olga had spent many happy days in the summer. Olga was presently enjoying new sights in Copenhagen with her parents, so for her, time might have passed faster than it did for Folke, but they would soon be united again. But who could ever expect that two months would pass so excruciatingly slowly?

Folke reported on the continuing strike in Gothenburg. There had not been any uprisings yet except for a protest against the trams being run by strike breakers. The mill owners (there were many textile and saw mills in Gothenburg at that time) had placed guards outside their mills and at the posh Särö, the well-to-do people had guards watching out for reprisals against their fine houses.

Folke and his father had arranged to have four guards outside the saw mill where they manufactured wood for export to Britain. Folke's father was also worried about a possible sabotage on the local train between Gothenburg and Särö.

Folke tells Olga he has discussed how to get servants for their household and they seem to be getting at least one servant who wants to get away from her harsh employer, a Mrs. Dickson, of a well known wealthy family of Scottish descent.

```
August 5, 1909
Olga Mims Dawson
c/o This Cook & Son
Copenhagen, Denmark
```
My own Dearest, Dearest "Älskling" (Darling), Olga Dear, thanks awfully much for your dear postcard which I received this morning. How I was longing to hear something from you.

Olga, it's hard, very hard indeed to be so far away from you. What cannot happen when you are so far away. Write me every day, if you cannot write a letter, write me a postcard. I'm so ledsen (sad) but it can't be helped.

Dear, how I wished to have you by my side. One minute only I should be satisfied. When I went to bed yesterday at Särö, I took your photograph with me from the veranda and when I went to bed and looked on it, I felt as if my heart should burst.

Dear, hope you are in Copenhagen and I'm indeed sorry that you all missed the boat, but at the same time, nothing bad, only if I had known that, I should have liked to stay with you that night in Malmö.

Papa was not a bit angry with me having gone that long way, he was only glad to have me back.

Nothing to do in the office, everything is lying in sleep. I went out by the 2.30PM train yesterday to Särö and then had dinner with aunt Axeline (Carlsson), my cousins and father, but how lonely I felt and I went through all the rooms to try to find you my dear. I went out in the garden with Toy (the dog) but not even he could make me glad and after that I took a walk with father just only for half an hour. Everything quiet and dead at the lawn tennis courts and all the visitors from the continent are away.

Aunt Axeline and all miss you all and we talked about you all the whole afternoon. Uncle Oscar is at Marstrand.

The strike is in its full blossom but no fights except the police cleared a market yesterday night where about three to four thousand people tried to stop the tramways. Only one line of the tramways has been stopped.

All the mill owners are guarding their mills with special watchmen and we have four all day and night. At Särö, a special guard is organized to look after the houses during the nights.

Hope there will be an end on all these troubles, I don't like them a bit.

It's a pity that you left Särö just when the fine weather came. My father told me they didn't have one drop of rain during the whole week and yesterday we had a glorious day. Dear, the sea was like a mirror, but I couldn't find you and I went on like in a dream.

You are with me but it's not the same. Two

mornings without having you to meet in the afternoon. The best thing is not to think of it. Only to think of October, but think Dear, more than two whole months.

I will finish up this letter after having had my tea, but I felt as if I could talk with you the whole day long.

Olga Dear, my father asked to write you that a good hotel in Berlin is Hotel Bristol, a first class hotel and one of the best and cheap too as there is no difference to talk about, in the prices in the German hotels.

In Wiesbaden, my father recommends Hotel Bellevue, a nice hotel for families and you get room and food for about ten marks a day if you are alone but if you are a family of course, you can get the prices reduced.

Hope you got my lettre addressed to Cook and also forwarded letters. Today I have forwarded some letters, newspapers and a parcel note from Cappelen and I hope you get it all right.

Ask in every town you come to at Cooks if they have offices in the next town where you are leaving for. I don't think they have got it in all the places. Let me know where to send them, if not. It's no trouble for you "min lilla älskling" (my little darling).

I'm going to see Mr. Fromell between 1 and 2AM today as he has something to tell me, he said so on the telephone this morning. I'll write you if anything interesting.

Philip Kraffts father came to visit father yesterday afternoon and he told me Philip had received Una's postcard all right. I'm going to have dinner at 3PM with Philip to arrange with him about some shooting (hunting) grounds we have together.

Dear, I hope you don't think I'm awful, I smoked one cigarette and one pipe yesterday. That's not mycket (much), is it?

Papa includes a card for you, hope you can read it. Papa is really very afraid that the workmen strikes shall make some mischiefs, for example, put some dynamite under the train or something like it, so he asked me to come with him in the last car of the train this morning (the train from Särö to Gothenburg).

Dear, I have talked over the servants matter with my father and our Maria and she knows Mrs. Dickson's servants and one of them doesn't want to stay any longer there and wanted to, I think, to come to us. She asked if you are a kind girl and not like Mrs. Dickson, who is not nice to her servants. I told Maria to tell her that I don't think the servants can get a kinder Madame than you my Dear.

Papa told me that he can easily let Maria come to us if we like it, do you like that Dear? Maria wants to come to us and she is the best we can get, but I haven't decided anything, only suggestions -- what do you think?

I suppose you have a fine time in Copenhagen and are glad to be able to see some museums which you didn't have time with in Stockholm.

Have not yet paid a visit to our flat but I think I will do that after 5PM if I don't go to Särö. At Särö, it is like a grave when I can´t find you there. But cheer up Folke, the two months must pass like an express train passes the telegraph poles. Hope you wish the same.

My grandmother wrote to Papa that she couldn't cry when she saw you and me -- she also wrote that she laughed long after we had left. She likes to see young people happy.

I am jealous of Mr. Lundberg (at the office). He telephones to his fiancée (in Sweden) the whole day and what can I do? I cannot telephone to you as very risky to get you on, but I wished you telephoned me. Can you do it tomorrow at let us say, between 10 and 2? I will stop at the office during that time.

Dear, give my very best regards to your Dear

father and mother, Una and Willie. You can tell them that I miss them very much and believe Dear you have the best parents you can wish.

Olga dear, I suppose you cannot get through half of this uninteresting letter, but never mind. I hug you and press you to my heart and some long kisses x--- x--- x--- x--- to my own little darling.

Think sometimes on your little loving, your own ever Folke

Hope Una is quite well. All at home send their very best regards to all.

AUGUST 6, 1909

Olga has written how much she and her family enjoyed Copenhagen, and we also learn that a family friend, Mrs. Berthelot has offered to have their wedding reception in her Paris flat. This is welcomed by Folke. It seems from his comment that this lady did not approve of Folke initially. Exactly what she objected to is not clear.

Olga, her mother and her siblings, had lived in Brussels and Paris for the last four years. The children had gone to school there continuously without going back to Jacksonville in Florida, so the Dawsons had made many friends both in Brussels and Paris, Mrs. Berthelot, being one of them. An American lady Mrs. Marshall, figures later in Olga's correspondence. Mrs. Marshall was of great help with the formalities and practical aspects of the wedding arrangements in Paris.

In Gothenburg the strike was still on and now the trams are no longer running. No violence yet, but some harmless explosions.

Folke also visited Olga and Folke's new flat which is situated on Sten Sturegatan 25 (it's still there) in Gothenburg. He was also taking care of some of the furnishing for the flat and reports on the progress to Olga. Olga surprised Folke by telephoning from Copenhagen and that sent Folke into seventh heaven.

August 6, 1909
Dearest, Dearest "lilla älskling" (little darling)
Thanks very very much for your two nice letters from Copenhagen. They reached me this morning and I read them over and over again. I am thinking of you day and night my dear little girl so far away from her "little baby", of course your own and nobody else's.

I'm so glad that you and your family are enjoying your trip and I fully agree with you that Copenhagen is a glamorous town and chic at the same time. Cheap also, hope you collected a little china vase from Copenhagen.

Thanks for the letter from Madame Berthelot (the family friend in Paris). That's very kind of her to take all the trouble and I have nothing to object at all of marrying in her home as we can make up with her and show her that she was wrong in her opinion about me.

I'm not quite sure if you will get this lettre all right but hope you find it. I went to see Mr. Fromell (Swedish man with an interest in Olga's sister Una) after having posted your lettre and he was as pleased to have received a postcard from your sister Una. I really think he is very fond of her, he shined like the sun when I told him what we had been doing in Stockholm.

After half an hour stay at the bank I left him to see Philip and we went together to see our flat because I have to give the store where we bought the copper pots, a measure of the oven.

I wished you could have gone with me, but no, you couldn't. We went also to the furniture store and asked them to alter the chairs a little and I also took the measurement of the beds for the pillow cases. After that I went alone and gave the shop the measurement, you know the one where you bought the corset cover.

How clever you must be, another cover. I am sure, not quite, that you will not have that finished before I see you again. You will have so much to see now in Germany and with packing and travelling you will get so tired. You cannot stop very long time in each place I suppose. I am interested in everything my Dear so you can tell me everything which happens on your way. I'm not going to tire you with 20 pages as I suppose you have no time to read the letter trough.

I went out to Särö as usual and looked at the tennis play a little while but that's not interesting. I can't find anything interesting but you my own little Darling.

The girl with the black hair came down to me on the tennis court and asked how I felt being a "grass-widower" (without partner) and I nearly cried. I only told her that I can't yet understand being away from my fiancée so long time.

When I went home, I passed the back door of your pavilion (Olga's family had rented three rooms and a balcony there during the summer) and I nearly went in and asked for Miss Olga, but went on my way home to the veranda.

I stopped at home talking over matters with my father and 10 minutes before we were to have supper, Philip came and joined us at the table. I followed him out to see some girls, the sister to the lieutenant who had something with his back this summer, but Dear, I couldn't stay more than an hour. I excused myself and went home.

Aunt Axeline was in town and hadn't come back yet so father, my cousins and I started playing a game of cards and we didn't even stop when aunt Axeline came home at 10PM, we continued to play up to 11.30PM when I was glad to go to bed and dream of you my Dear.

Father has not gone to town today either as there is not much to do here, everything is stopped, even all the tramways have begun to strike today so we have to walk to and from the railway station (Linneplatsen), but I think it's very good for the health to have some miles to walk every day. No fires or something like that except some men had put some detonating caps in front of the tramcars, so it sounded like a bomb, but no damages.

Dearie, one pipe and one cigarette yesterday so you can see I am not smoking very much. I will try to reduce the smoking altogether one day, I can do everything for you.

Write me if you received this letter all right, but hope so. You leave (for Berlin) first tomorrow morning my Dear. I cannot tell you how glad I was, I was so glad, so glad, to hear your voice on the telephone that I could hardly speak. Now when I have talked to you, you my own Dear, how I miss you. You will find this letter uninteresting more than ever.

The life is not worth very much without you, for me not so "mycket" (much) as the weight of a hair. The sun is shining and I think you can see the same sun, but I cannot, but you are "tout seul" (completely alone) in my heart, min lilla älskling (my little sweetheart).

I suppose my Dear that you are tired to read my writing any longer so will close.

My little Darling, I could cry when I think I have you so far away and will you take these dry x-------- x-------- x-------- x-------- long kisses.

So long Dearie, my very best regards to your family, but receive first of all another kiss as thanks for your nice idea, was it yours, to telephone. <u>You didn't know how good I felt after having heard your little voice.</u>

Dearie, lots of kisses from your always loving, longing ever, ever your baby Folke

August 7, 1909

The days passed very slowly for Folke since there is no work to be done as long as the strike is going on. The days probably passed a lot faster for Olga who was busy travelling. Folke asks Olga how she likes Berlin as the family has left Copenhagen and are spending a week in Berlin.

Folke mentions that he has reduced his smoking. Olga has asked him not to smoke more than three cigarettes a day as she dislikes this unhealthful habit. This topic is ongoing in their correspondence as we have already noticed.

The Dawsons have left Copenhagen and the letters are now addressed to Cooks in Berlin.

```
August 7, 1909
Olga Mims Dawson
Weltreiseburau Union
Cooks Correspondents
Berlin
Germany
```
Dearest, Dearest Olga!
Not very much to write about but I feel I must speak a little with you.

The days pass slowly, very slowly and nothing can interest me. I don't like a bit going to Särö. Yesterday I went out at 5.30PM and Papa didn't come home before 9PM. He returned from a fishing excursion with aunt Axeline (Carlsson) and my cousin. Altogether they brought home 85 fish. That's very good.

How do you like Berlin? I have never visited that town, but from pictures I can understand same being quite a nice town.

Dear my own Olga, I am doing nothing here, I could easily have been able to travel with you all around Germany. Papa is not in town either. He simply takes his holidays.

I could also stay out at Särö, but Dear "min Älskling" (my Darling), I travel with pleasure down to town (the office) every day to look for letters from you, that's my only pleasure since you left me.

You are lucky my dear to be able to travel like you do. I went to bed at 9.30PM yesterday as nothing interested me.

Yesterday I smoked two cigarettes. You can see that I'm reducing the allowed three.

My Dear Dear little Olga, if you knew how much I love you my Darling. I miss you dreadfully. I return the letter from Mrs. Berthelot.

Hope to hear from you tomorrow. I close for today and give my kindest regards to your family.

Dearest, Dearest on the earth, I kiss you x-----x----x----x----x---- and a little "pourboire"

Always your loving, longing ever
Folke

August 8, 1909

The days pass extremely slowly for Folke and a letter arrives that has Folke quite confused. Olga suggests that maybe their marriage is a bit hasty, and that they need more than two months to decide. I think this is just Olga thinking aloud wanting reassurance, and not seriously considering a delay. Also, she is all alone with her thoughts. If she and Folke had been able to be together such doubts would not have crept into her mind. To Folke, any more waiting would have been sheer torture. One must not forget that Olga was eighteen, still only a teenager and had not been told anything about was goes on in a marriage. She was truly innocent. She will however return to this subject later in their correspondence.

Olga is to give Folke a wedding gift, as they must have discussed preciously, in the form of a gentleman's travel toiletry case. To make it easier, Folke offers to buy it himself if she is not able to get her father to buy it before he starts his journey.

Olga has asked Folke if he shows her letters to anyone else, but he confirms that they are kept private.

August 8, 1909
Dearest, Dearest my own Älskling,
How are you today. Hope quite well. It's Sunday, and if the other days have been hard, this is quite dreadful. I simply don't know what to do. I'm walking about in the garden and looking for you, but can't find you.

I feel like if you should come in the room every minute. Dearie, I'm sitting writing in the salon but no piano-playing by my little baby. It's nothing to do here, so I'm going in to town tonight, but will wait for the 7.30PM train.

I went out to Särö yesterday at 11AM as Hjalmar and Ruth (Folke's sister and her husband) came out after having made the nice trip through the canal and all around the south of Sweden. They were quite delighted with their journey and had had most beautiful weather.

Before dinner, Hjalmar and I took a little sailing and after dinner we went out fishing a little. I caught 17 fish, Martin 5 and Hjalmar none as he was too lazy to fish and slept during the time we were fishing.

After supper we played a game of cards and Dear, I do everything mechanically as my thoughts are with you and nowhere else. When I was out fishing, I did not enjoy it one bit as the fun is finished without you.

Dearie, I'm counting the days and they go very slowly! I have just been down to the station to see Hjalmar and Ruth off, they left for Axvall. They asked me to give you and your family their very best regards.

The man from the office told me that he had forwarded a letter to me. Haven't yet received it, but I expect it's from you my Dear. He also forwarded some cards or letters for you. I asked him to do so.

We have the most glorious weather today and I can't understand why we always had such bad weather when your father was here.

Have just received your kind sweet letter and if you could see how glad I was, you can understand Dear how I have been looking for it. Thanks Dearest.

Dear, how silly of Fromell. Did he propose to Una. Dear, believe me, I didn't know a bit that he had written my Dear. He only asked me for Una's address and I told him Cooks. I thought he only would thank for the postcard.

Dear what do you mean by two months being too soon? You don't want to postpone the marriage do you?

Dear, don't press upon your father with the 'valise' (a gentleman's fancy toiletry travelling case in fine leather), because if he can't buy it now, I can always get it later. You can write me only a week before I leave Gothenburg (for the wedding in Paris) if you can give it to me. That's all.

Why do you ask me how in the world you wrote such a long letter? If you knew how I like to talk to you and <u>receive reply</u>, you wouldn't ask me. You can answer me just as long, but Dear don't write me when you don't feel inclined to do so.

I cannot possibly get this letter posted tonight here at Särö as I want it to go by tonight's tram (the trams had post office mailboxes attached and they were emptied when the trams passed the central post office downtown) from Gothenburg so I will leave here tonight and post it in Gothenburg.

Dear, don't think that I have my thoughts anywhere else than with you, and for you. Never. Never.

I smoked one pipe and one cigarette yesterday.

Dear write me what Fromell said, he is silly. I am not telling a soul a word of what you write to me in private.

I am quite sure that you will be ready for October, won't you? You know your own little baby is waiting for you, waiting with patience, but it's long for me, very long.

Papa, Auntie, and Atterboms (Folke's sister Ruth and husband Hjalmar) and my cousins give their kindest regards to you all.

Write me soon and take care of yourself my Dear and think sometimes of me.

There's some x------x-----x----- my Dear and I am always your own longing, loving ever Folke

August 9, 1909

Folke writes that the strike is still going on. All is calm, absolutely nothing is going on and that makes the days pass even more slowly. Folke's father, Axel is using the time to have a well deserved vacation. The details for the wedding in Paris are not definite and Folke has a suggestion, one of many that the young couple will discuss. As Olga and Folke come from two different countries, America and Sweden, and they will be married in a third country, France, and Folke is Lutheran and Olga, Catholic, which means that there are many formalities that must be observed and documents to be procured and translated -- not an easy task. Olga and Folke's correspondence during August and September deals with many of these matters and what strikes me is how fluid their plans were, until very close to the actual wedding on October 18, 1909.

August 9, 1909
Dearest, Dearest my own Olga,
Another day passed and another day without you my Dear. How I love you and look forward to

October when I can go down to the station and take the train for Paris.

Strike still here and nothing serious has happened. All the striking workmen have made a demonstration today but so far, everything calm. The worse thing about the strike and lockout, is that the workmen who want to work, dare not, they are afraid to be killed or smashed to pieces.

I came to town yesterday night and went to post your letter and returned to our flat, I mean Papas flat at 9PM. I went straight to bed after having taken a refreshing bath. Dear I smoked three cigarettes yesterday (Sunday). Today at 2PM, nothing so far.

I can't get rid of thinking of Fromell, he must have been mad if he proposed to Una. Dear, if you are going to stop in Berlin one whole week, are you then going to visit Dresden and Leipzig? Have you time for that? You need time to get your trousseau ready.

I have nothing to do here at the office so I'll take a "cat nap" a while as I'll wait for the afternoon mail and hope to hear something from you.

My dear, Aunt Axeline asked me to thank you so much for your sweet letter to her and also Papa for Una's letter.

Dear, how I miss you all, I wished I had travelled with you as here everything is sleeping, no tramcars, no taxis-autos, no cabs, no work in our mill -- with one word "nothing".

Tomorrow it's my mother's Death Day so I'll go out to her grave and put some flowers. Papa will certainly come to town tomorrow but he is still taking his holidays and no wonder, nothing to do for him here, and for the second, he needs badly a rest and luckily it's glorious sunshine every day.

Yes Dear, I'm always thinking of you when I see the beautiful sunsets we have now every day. Simply wonderful. My thoughts are running to you "min lilla älskling" (my little darling) and I never, never can understand that I could live without you. You are everything to me and you are the only one who can make me happy, both at the moment and in whole my life.

I'll do my very best to be the best husband and you will see my dear that if we both do so, we will never have any quarrels or disputes. We will then live a happy life. Don't you think so min lilla rara älskling (my sweet little darling)?

Dear, I'm not quite sure that this is quite according to the law, but Papa has promised me to ask a lawyer if your religion (Catholic) allows for us to be married at the Swedish legation in Paris. I think the Swedish (Lutheran) minister is permitted to marry us. His name is Count Gyldenstolpe and we could then also have the American minister as a witness. Afterwards, they could be invited for lunch or something like it, to Madame Berthelot and we will never have to go to the "Palais de Justice".

Think over the matter and in the meantime I'll get information about what is according to the law. Don't talk very much about this to your parents, write to Madame Marshall first and ask her if you can do so or if you want any special papers. Please write soon about the papers so we can be sure to get them if you want any.

Dear, take everything coolly with your trousseau. You will have everything ready in time. I'm quite sure. Won't you my Dear?

I'm longing for you so very much Dear. The mail arrived but no letter from you my Dear. Nothing today. Dearie, my own Darling, take care of yourself and if you want, there are some long x---- x----- x---- x---- kisses.

All send their regards to you all.

Lot's of love from your loving, longing always your Folke

August 10, 1909

Folke's letters to Olga are still addressed to Berlin. Folke mentions how he and his father have been to his mother's grave since it was her "Death Day" as he called it in his previous letter.

Folke's beautiful mother Ragnhild had died from diabetes 6 years earlier, only thirty-nine years old. The grave was at the "Örgryte Old Church" dating back hundreds of years and, from the grave, at that time, Folke and his father would have been able to look across some fields were cows probably grazed, at the reasonably new apartment blocks on Sten Sturegatan, where at number 25, Olga and Folke's new flat was situated. The same building is still there today.

Folke tells Olga that he plans to participate in a sailing race at Särö and enter his boat "Olga". Also, Folke has to make many of the decisions of how to furnish the new flat since Olga is not there.

August 10, 1909
My own Dearest Olga,
Dear, hope you are all right, but I'm really afraid as no letter yesterday and none today. The only hope I have is to receive some news from you my Dear with the next mail coming in at 4PM. I understand that you have very little time to spare for writing as you have the whole family to attend to and a lot to visit and to look at.

Hope you enjoyed your trip and have such nice weather as we still have, heat and a bright blue sky the whole day. Dear, the days are very long, very long.

Papa and I have come back to the office just an hour ago from my dear mother's grave and it was so pretty and peaceful there.

We also passed our future home, my own "lilla älskling". Won't it be curious to come to your own home. Have been today and looked at some curtains but have not decided anything thereabout.

On Monday next, we will have a race between Särö sailing boats and I'm thinking to try to sail our boat "Olga". Hope to win a prize, it will always increase the cups we are going to have to have around our dining room. Will write you further about this race if I'm going to join it.

Have just returned from dinner and no letter. Dear, I hope you are all right. My kindest regards to everybody.

I am always your own loving ever
Folke

AUGUST 11, 1909

Olga always sent her letters to the office of Jonsson & Sternhagen but this time she has sent a letter to Särö which brightens Folke's day no end.

The strike is on and there has been a fire of some kind, which has affected the energy of Folke's father and his nerves especially. Normally insurance companies do not cover fires during strikes, but Folke has contacted an English insurance company which might be willing to cover this risk -- at a very high premium no doubt.

Folke is sweet and loving in saying that he can easily read Olga's terrible handwriting. He can read her every word he reassures her -- as though written on a typewriter. He loves her letters and wants nothing to discourage her from writing to him. Folke sends his special regards to Olga's mother who has been most supportive to the young couple and has, indeed, made the marriage possible.

Folke had picked a rose, pressed and kissed it and put it in the letter for Olga to kiss it too. Olga loved it and responded that she would keep it for ever. She did. It is still in the envelope today. Over a hundred years later, the pressed rose is faded, but it has been kissed many times by both Olga and Folke.

The envelope was addressed to Weltreiseburau
Union
Cooks Correspondents
Berlin but was forwarded to Dresden

```
August 11, 1909
Dearest, Dearest "älskling",
```
Your long sweet letter to hand yesterday. When I came out to Särö, you should have seen me. I came up to the veranda stairs, found the door locked, but I could see your letter on the table. I rushed to the side door and read your letter, yes, read it more than four times and enjoyed every word. Yes, Dearie, I was so very afraid that something had happened to you. Thanks <u>very,</u> <u>very</u> much for it. I was so sad in the train going out to Särö, but I was another man when I got your letter. I didn't know you had written it to the Särö address.

Since I've written you yesterday, my father told me that his doctor has advised him to change air and take some rest and consequently he has gone to Marstrand and will remain there some days. His nerves are not quite all right and you can understand that the fire and the strike have taken a lot of his strength. He is also afraid of the new mill, that some young socialists will put fire again on the mill and if there is a revolt and a dire, we wont get anything from the insurance companies. I have today got an English company who probably want to take the risk of the mill during the strike, so that will make Papa better if I can get that settled.

Dearie, I'm enjoying me as well as I can do and believe me, I don't think "me held under any promise", but I can't alter what my heart feels for you. Without you, I can't live. I'm quite sure of it and the two months will soon pass I hope and then I hope of the whole of my heart, that I shall find my little Olga quite the same girl as I've always found her. She won't run away with someone else. Will she?

Dear I'm always yours and couldn't change for anything on earth. You know it and don't think I'm only writing so. I write with the whole of my heart and Dearie, don't think "Silly boy he is in love", that's true, but not silly love. I wouldn't have asked you to marry me if I hadn't meant it.
Dearie, I'm so glad you like the Hotel and hope you will find the Bellvue in Wiesbaden just as nice. I haven't seen Berlin but have always heard that it is a nice town. Glad you found Mr. Deerings so nice; yes I like him very much and have known him since I was a little kid of fourteen.
Olga, I write in every letter how many cigarettes I've smoked, but today, no smoking at all and I'll try to smoke then and then when I feel inclined and try to let several days pass without anything so I can be strong and live long with you.
Dearie, a man should never do anything against the one he loves.
Yes Dearie, I can read every word you write, quite every word of your letters and dont think that I can't do it. I'm now used to your writing, just like it was written on a typewriter (sweet to say, but Olga's handwriting was very difficult to read, and still is).
I'll take your advice and read an English book, it's good for my English and it kills time. I better go to town every day. Days pass quicker and also there is always some little thing in the office to attend to. Also better ink and paper. You know how bad it is to write in the salon. Hope you can read every word of what

I write or get the head meaning of it, as I'm quite sure you have trouble in understanding my bad English and wrong spelling.

The strike still in it's full blossom and we only get a funny newspaper, only a little typewritten page with the most important news. These are strange times we are living in.

My brother Axel in London (he studied there) was coming over here for his holidays on Monday but we telegraphed him to postpone them as there is no pleasure to come over during troubles like these.

Toy (the dog) is so good and nice and he misses you. I'm quite sure of it.

Hope your dear mother is quite well. Give her my special best regards. She has been so good and nice to us. I'll never forget it. She has helped me to my happiness, I'm quite sure.

Fromell telephoned me and asked how I was, and asked me to come down to see him in the bank one day, but Dear, be sure I won't tell him a word that I know what he had written to Una. How silly of him, he had only met her four or five times and then to write such a stupid letter.

I went out last night with Philip (Krafft) and the two sisters to the lieutenant and we sat down talking for nearly an hours on the rocks near the "Herr bad" (men's bathhouse at Särö) you know. The night was so beautiful and the ciel (sky) was so full of bright stars. I sat quite some minutes thinking of you my Dear. The youngest of the girls is very nice. She was a bridesmaid on one of my cousins wedding last year. She is very fond of my brother with the big head (must be Folke's brother Axel).

Yes Dearie, the Krafft girl is engaged to Mr. Lindström, they are going to marry in the beginning of September and are now looking for a flat. They told me they can't possibly find one and then I gave them the address of Fromell's flat, but perhaps it's already taken.

   I took the rose you will find on this letter yesterday and pressed it and kissed it. I hope you will kiss it too.
   Dearie, I miss you more and more every day. Take care of yourself älskling (darling). No Dear, I've not forgotten my promise to send you a profile photo, but I've not taken it yet, but will take it today at Särö and brush my hair up as you like it and send it on to you as fast as possible. I've said to myself every day, go today, no tomorrow, today, no next day. You understand. Excuse me.
   It was funny yesterday, my American second cousin telephoned me and asked me to buy some bacon and marmalade and I did it so you can understand I've already begun the home shopping.
   Dear, everybody thank you for your kind regards to them and send theirs back to you all. We are talking the whole time about you and I talk English not to forget the little I can.
   Hope you are all quite well, as we are and give my love to your Papa, Mama, sister Una and Willie and take the very best for yourself and some long x------------- x-------------- kisses and let me soon hear from you, my own little älskling (little darling).
   I am always your loving little "baby" ever Folke

PS I'm going out to Särö now at 2.30PM and will try to fish after having taken the photo. I dream about you my Darling and I can see you wherever I look.

AUGUST 12, 1909
This is one of Folke's shorter letters and a relief to me who has to copy them into the computer, but I

shouldn't say such a thing, I will miss Folke and Olga and their life in the distant past when there are no more letters...

Folke tells Olga that he has played tennis which he does not do too often it seems and Olga later replied that tennis was *"good for a lovesick boy"*.

August 12, 1909
Miss Olga Dawson
This Cook & Son
Dresden, Germany

Dearest, Dearest Olga,
Thanks very much for your kind postcard.

Dear, don't address your letters or p.c to Särö as I'm not going out there every night as Mr. Lundberg will soon leave office for some time and I have to attend to business.

Dear, would you believe, I had a photograph taken yesterday and hope it will be all right. In the afternoon I played a game with the two sisters of the lieutenant. Would you believe that I played tennis.

My little cousin is going to Stockholm today at 12AM and I will see her off.

Dear, I'm longing so for you, but you are so far away, further away for each day. Just a second to talk with you, I would be so thankful.

Already the 12th, soon only one and a half months left. Dearie, when you can fix the date, I would be glad to know it, just about three days difference, that doesn't matter.

All send their kindest regards to you all. Hope you are quite well and I send you my own little älskling, the best wishes for you to be quite well, happy and for a nice time.

Kisses x----- x----- to you my Darling from your own longing, loving ever
Folke

AUGUST 13, 1909

Olga is still in Dresden and in this letter, Folke calls her "Mimsie" for the first time, a diminutive of her middle name Mims (an old family name).

Olga collects little vases and has sent a drawing of the various vases she has collected. She will have a nice flat waiting to place them in. Folke thinks that Olga shouldn't exhaust herself getting vases from every city.

Folke reports that the strike is still on, but the workers were beginning to back to work. The strike was losing its momentum since the unions were not strong enough in those days. They did not have enough funds in their coffers for a strike, besides the unions had been forced to strike because of the lockout, it was not a strike they had themselves planned.

Olga has written a letter to Folke who has a great need to talk to Olga every day and so he writes a lot, much more than she does. He once wondered if his letters wore her out and Olga replied about his letters: *"They are read, not once, but many times at night, the last thing and the first thing in the morning. I know what a sincere hand has written them and what a true, pure heart, has dictated them"*

August 13, 1909
My Dearest Mimsie,
Thanks very very much for your sweet kind long letter. I read it over and over again my Darling so I know it nearly by heart.

Don't walk too much about in the towns to find the vases, it's not good for you my Dear and besides it's not absolutely necessary to have one from <u>every</u> town.

I'm so happy that you will put the marriage in the beginning of October as I'm longing after you. Wherever I go I look for you and specially out at Särö, all the places have some memories. The little room where you always used to comb your hair. All places in the garden. I can see you everywhere but it's not reality -- what's the good then? Yes, it's good when you think about the one you love.

I invited Philip (Krafft) for dinner yesterday at Särö and afterwards we asked the two girls you know, the sisters, out for a fishing picnic but unfortunately, as soon as the anchor was thrown out, the oldest of them asked to take it up again and go home as she was afraid for rain and storm. When we came ashore, we went out for a walk in the country but I felt tired when we came home. I think it was the company. Dear, if you would have been with me, I wouldn't have felt tired.

I went early to bed yesterday and came in to town by the 12.15AM train and will remain here till morning as it is a storm and nothing to do at Särö.

Owing to the strike, nothing has been done in our flat, but it will not take more than a fortnight when they begin.

I'm arranging everything in the flat so when you come, you can only alter which you don't think is nice. I'm looking forward to when I'll open the door and ask you to step in. Dear, won't it be glorious?

Excuse me that my handwriting is bad but I've to hurry on as the train with the foreign mail leaves in half an hour and you will probably have left Dresden if I wait to mail it.

Dearie, thank Una for her postcard and first of all, you shall have thanks for your two cards from Berlin.

On Monday afternoon I'll get the photos and will then send you the cards and you can chose which you like and which you want me to order.

I've settled the insurance business so we will probably start our mill on Monday or Tuesday. The strikes continues but the workmen begin to go back to their work more and more for every day. No fights yet, but it's only calm before the storm.

Yes Dearie, I showed my little cousin the furniture yesterday and she will probably make us a cover for the dining room or for the smoking room. She liked them very much and thought we had a very good taste and how wonderful to chose them in an hour she said.

Give your father, mother and Una and Willie, my best regards. Aunt Axeline asked me to give her kindest regards to all of you.

I'll now go and do some small commissions for aunt A. and then have dinner. Monday or Tuesday I'll go out shooting if the strike continues as then there is nothing to do.

Now I feel inclined to work but can't get any work. Darling, take care of yourself and hurry on with your trousseau.

I'm waiting for you my Dear and to leave for Paris, it will be the happiest time. You can still and always have the hope that I have reduced my smoking. One pipe a day or one or two cigarettes a day, that's all.

My little älskling, good buy, so long and I'm always your own true loving, longing little "baby" Folke

AUGUST 14, 1909
The days pass very slowly, especially with the strike still on.

August 14, 1909
My dearest Mimsie,
Thanks in heaps for your kind postcard. Dearie, I'm so lonesome without you. I stopped in town yesterday and went very early to bed, only to let the time pass quicker. I sat by the window and thought that if you had been here, I would never have felt so lonely.

The days pass, just one like the other, the only excitement is when your sweet letters arrive.

It's now the third day running it's blowing very hard. Full storm, so I don't think I'll risk my life tomorrow in sailing. Then I wouldn't be able to marry you Darling.

I can see you standing by me Dear, your soul is with me, or is it your heart? I have it, n'est-ce pas? Darling, I'm longing so after you.

The tea came in now, I'll have some now and will continue afterwards.

Papa just came home from Marstrand and will go to Särö with me.

The workmen in our mill will probably begin working on Monday. Always very good, as there is nothing to do.

Aunt Axeline will write to you but she'll wait until you come to Paris.

Dearie, good buy for now. I'll continue tomorrow and write you as I must out to Särö. Love to all from us.

Dearie, take the very best care for yourself from your longing, loving, ever, your true little "baby" Folke

AUGUST 15, 1909

Folke spent a lonely Sunday out at Särö and the letter is therefore a long one. Olga's response to this long letter was. *"Wonderful for a foreigner to write a twenty-four page note. Why marvellous!"*

Folke writes very charmingly how they will keep their house filled with flowers and make their home beautiful together. No wonder that Olga's mother promoted this marriage. Where could Olga have found a more suitable man?

Folke's temperament is different from Olga's who reflects on their separation as an *"opportunity to find out if they have made any mistake"*. She tells Folke to *"have fun and not be bound to any promises"*.

But what about her asking Folke not to smoke more than three cigarettes and not to drink alcohol? Not so logical, dear Olga.

It seems that Folke did not want to chance anything before the wedding, no doubt knowing that people can do silly things if they drink alcohol. He has therefore not tasted alcohol since he was engaged. It was a promise he gave to Olga. Considering that Folke as an older man, was a true gourmand and loved his brandy and cigarettes, agreeing to this sacrifice, shows how totally dedicated the young Folke was to marrying her. No sacrifice was too great to secure her as his wife.

August 15, 1909
Dearest, dearest Älskling,
My very best thanks for your letter, not yet to hand, but I'll get it out to this little isle at 5PM as the man (at the office) has forwarded it to me this morning.

Dearie, another Sunday and I've to go alone here and my thoughts are with you, my heart away travelling with my little Mimsie. It's very hard to see all the engaged people here at Särö. They are together and I've to be separated from you my darling.

Anyhow, I take it as a man and believe me, this separation has made my love to you still more stronger min lilla älskling (my little darling).

Yesterday when we came out to Särö, Mr. Blidberg asked Papa and me to come and have a game of bridge at his villa. We went to him at 6.30PM and played up to 11PM with an interval for supper. His wife played also with us. You know the family, it's my tailor.

He offered me whisky and I laughed and said, "Oh no, spirit for me" and told him that I hadn't tasted alcohol since I was engaged.

I had bad luck in the cards as I lost most of

the games, but not so heavy, 3,85 kronor. Perhaps I couldn't follow the game as my thoughts were running in another direction. Yes indeed they were.

I slept rather late this morning and went out after breakfast to look at the race with the sailing boats. I didn't join it as I thought there was not a chance of winning as we have not enough sail for our boat. Anyhow, the race is finished and all of them arrived safely.

Yes my Dear, if you had been here, the day would have been more interesting than it was. I'm wishing the day was over as I'm always one day nearer October when I will meet you, you, everything in my whole life.

Isn't love a wonderful old thing? Excuse the blot on the other side, but it's a kiss to you. I actually got it on the letter when I moved up to my room as my father came home with two of his friends from Gothenburg and I wanted to write my little letter to you älskling alone and not with a lot of talk around.

The day is so wonderful and the birds are singing so beautifully. I would really like to be a bird for a few days, I know where I would fly, right to Germany where my darling is and I would sit by her and sing.

Has your mother decided anything for herself, where is she going to stay during the winter? It is unnecessary for me to tell you -- whatever she wants me to do here, would be a pleasure as I can never give back what she has done for me.

I will now go down for dinner and continue this letter afterwards. I have no pleasure going down, but if you would have been here, I wouldn't have to be up here with my thoughts of my little darling in Germany.

I wished you could be here now. I'm not ledsen (sad), only longing after you, the one I love <u>so much</u> and mycket mer (much more).

Your sweet long letter reached me some minutes ago and Dear, I have read it as a happy boy can read a letter from a loving girl. I'm so happy to know you are thinking of me and if I could hug you I should do it the whole time my Darling, and Dearie, I can understand that you can't write me long letters every time as you must attend to your Dear family. You are so much wanted to help them.

Dearie, so nice that you got the vase from every town and the shapes are so nice (Olga has sent a drawing of them). Min kära Mimsie (My Dear Mimsie), the shape of mine is this (drawing enclosed).

As I have told you before in this letter, I didn't go in for the sailing race this time as no chance to winning whatever.

Yes Dearie, I love flowers, and so do you, and my idea is to have, if we can, flowers in every room and of course, <u>the two of us</u>, shall make <u>our</u> flat to something glorious. I myself alone can't, but with your small pretty hands, we must succeed. Yes Dear, I'm certain that you will make our flat pretty, not only with flowers. With you in the flat, the flat is so perfect.

I can only see Master Willie (Olga's younger brother) walking about with his camera. I remember myself when I got my first camera. I thought I was at least five years older. But now is the question, how long will that pleasure last for him. Hope a very long time. He will then have some things to attend to and leave min lilla älskling (my little darling) alone and let her buy her trousseau without a brother in her skirt to make her angry.

Dearie, your father's thanks to my father is accepted with every (can't find the word) but you know that my father has done every thing he can do to <u>please me</u>, so it is not only you, it's me nearly alone who must thank him for his hospitality as you call it.

Dearie, you ask me for papers. I have forwarded them together with several letters. Hope you will receive them.

Well dear, travel and enjoy yourself the one and a half months left until you marry me, but Dear, I like travelling just as much as you and and as much as we can afford to travel, we will do it, be sure of it. So many people have told me that especially your second wedding trip is the most glorious and perhaps they are right. About our trip, you can settle that when I come down to Paris. Either we go to London or Dover to the south.

Dearie, that's a good idea to buy part of your trousseau in Germany. Of course you can't get everything in Germany, you want your spare time also. That's very kind of your father to give you one thousand dollars for your trousseau.

No dear, my eyes will never be red of reading your writing or letters. Never, but certainly they would if I did not have them to read. Yes I'm sure.

Dearie, I know that your Dear father can't give you what he promised but that's nothing to think of, when he can give it to you, he'll do it and nothing more about that. It's you and not your money I want, and besides as you used to say, "My father has no money". I'll write you about the valise tomorrow.

I have not yet seen our flat in different colours, but I can fully understand that our home will be chic, yes indeed. We will collect and collect from different places, nice and beautiful things and after some years we can look back when we bought that and that.

Yes Dearie, I cannot think about our home, future life, without shining up. Won't it be glorious? Will write you tomorrow about other questions when I've been to the rug store and at the church to ask if we must announce the wedding in the church three Sundays before we marry.

Dearie, I wish I could continue to talk, but it is nearly seven. I'll take the 7.30 train.

Excuse the writing, but it's written out at Särö with a pen as a pin.

My father thanks very much for your kind regards and love, so also aunt Axeline. Both send their love to you all and hope you will remain healthy. Touch wood.

Dearie, min lilla älskling, kisses to tell you good night and sleep well wishes. Your loving, longing always Folke

AUGUST 16, 1909

Olga and her family are now in Cologne.

Folke has written a very long letter (36 pages) inspired by a long letter from Olga. She has told Folke to be careful with his spelling and has been a bit hard on him but he takes it in the best way possible. He has no intention of causing any ill feelings whatsoever. He is not risking anything.

Folke has a few practical things to arrange with the church in Sweden, and Olga has a few things to arrange at her end. The ongoing strike has affected the work on Olga and Folke's flat but it will be ready in good time for them to move into. The two of them had started setting up their home during the summer when Olga and her family visited -- the flat on Sten Sturegatan and many other practical matters arranged and furniture bought.

Grandmother Olga told me in later years, that she and Folke bought "sets" of furniture for the various rooms and apparently they decided on the furniture in an hour. It was only later, when they began reading design magazines that their taste developed and they replaced the early pieces. From their reading in "The Studio" art and design magazine, they had a local carpenter make medieval Tudor style furniture in oak.

Folke was very much involved in buying items for their homes and has specific suggestions for the silver cutlery and where to buy it. Folke took great delight in making their home just right for Olga. It is interesting to note that bed sheets were custom made in those days.

The strike is still on and the risk of losing the sawmill in a fire without adequate insurance has been averted by buying a special insurance policy from England at great expense. Folke's father, Axel Jonsson had to pay 11,000 British pounds for the insurance. An amazing amount of money for the times.

Olga has written about her trousseau: *"I've nearly compiled my underwear and will now begin on hats, dresses and coats. Things are made better in Germany than France"*. She prefers quality over quantity, has quite indulged herself and somewhat guiltily admits that she favours lace underwear. Folke points out that she will also need some heavier stuff too. He has just bought wood to keep the flat warm. He knows what Swedish winters are like.

```
August 16, 1909
Miss Olga Dawson
c/o This Cook & Son
Köln (Cologne), Tyskland
Dearest lilla Älskling Olga,
```
Another long letter on my desk this morning and a postcard also. Olga Dear, take some long kisses (you know how good they taste) as a little thanks for them both. I don't know how to thank you enough for them, I simply swallowed them.

Dearie, how I'm sorry to have written or rather spelled my letters so bad, but Dearie, I've not thought about the spelling, I've thought about <u>you</u>. But from now I'll think first of you, then also about the spelling. With a dictionary on the desk, I'll improve, at least try, but Dearie, I'm not angry, I'm thankful that you will have the trouble to tell me when my letters are too bad.

Dearie, I've just returned from the church expedition (administration) and they told me that I only need a "marriage certificate" and to complete that, you have to write me your full name, where you were born, the date and the year -- the lucky date of your birth.

Dearie, that's the only thing I need from you here and when I've got that, they will advertise it in the papers here three weeks before we marry. Can you give me answers on these three questions as soon as possible.

I think you had better go to an American consulate perhaps in Cologne and ask if you need any papers from America to marry a Swede of another religion than yours, so that you will have time to write and get the papers wanted, so we won't have to wait for them.

Will you trouble yourself with all these things. Perhaps the American consul can give you the papers, but I hardly think so, and we have not much time to spare.

Dearie, I await your kind reply to these questions. Certainly, my little älskling (darling) will have this trouble.

Dearie, the strike has put back the work with the flat, but Dearie, the owner of our future home told me that it will take about 10 days to make it all right.

I'll go and look at rugs today and will write you later when I've been there if I've time as I am going out shooting with two of my friends tonight and stay out all day tomorrow. I'll think of you and if we get some fowl I would like that you were here to try them.

Dearie, I've no wish whatever about the valise (Olga's gift to Folke), only to be filled with the most necessary things for me, not for an officer as he wants a lot of unnecessary things for his top boots and I have no use for shaving knives. Well Dearie, one valise well fitted with necessary things of this shape (rectangular drawing enclosed) with my name burned in. Not one of the larger, not one of the smallest, something in between. You know it. I'm sure. N'est-ce pas? If not, I will try to give more specifications.

Also, about what I'll spend on the flat -- can't possibly tell you as I've not bought all small things for servant hall, carpets, curtains etc. etc. As soon as I can give you near specification I'll do it if you want, but around 6,000 kronor to 6,500 without the piano.

Dearie, about the silver I think you, or rather we, need:
3 dozen large forks
2 dozen smaller forks
2 dozen large spoons
2 dozen smaller spoons
2 dozen the, eggs etc. spoons
3 dozen big knives
2 dozen small knives

The knives to fit the size of the forks. Hope you understand me, but Dearie, I only suggest you this, not if you think it too many, but think, if we have a dinner for twelve or eighteen persons, we need all these forks and knives. Or what do you say? Of course Dearie, they will put our initials on for nothing.

I think you get the best at the shop where we bought the silver frames.

What do you want for a wedding present from me? Tell me, I guess a diamond ring. N'est-ce pas?

I couldn't sleep last night, I was quite awake and thought of you, only of you. Dearie, what a pleasure to make your home nice and to go and look for everything you need. I only wish I had you by my side as I'm not so sure now when I've to choose things as when we were together and bought the furniture.

You don't know how many small things I have to buy. Here are only some: All the glasses for the table and all water carafes, knives and forks for the kitchen, bread knives, chairs for the same and all furniture for the servants rooms, baskets, bring wood to the flat (for burning in tiled ovens, "kakelugnar"), telephone and lots of other things. I could fill 20 pages with them.

When you can fix the date I should be pleased but first we must have your papers ready. What do you say about marrying for the ministers?

Dearie, you can have me quite for yourself. I shall be too pleased if you want me and true as gold will your "baby" be. Yes, he couldn't be untrue.

Dearie, I'm always keeping my hair straight up but of course when it is cut, it won't be still up as usual, but Dearie, I tell you, I'm not a mouse, playing about when the cat is away. How could you think so Dear? I'm the same when you are here or not, that's true.

Yes Särö is wonderful but my Darling, it's nothing for me at present, nothing but I remember every stone where we have been together and it makes my heart burst when I think that two months, no it's only one and a half months now, the time passes but slowly. At least for me.

Dearie, my father is now much better and he has arranged insurance of the mill against everything for British pounds 11,000, so he is quite safe if unluckily a fire should destroy the mill.

Aunt Axeline is still at Särö but will leave in some days and go to Marstrand. I'm not quite sure but almost.

Dearie, how could you think that I would be tired to be engaged to you for 8 whole years. Never Dear, I would and could go much longer and wait for you if we had to, but Dearie, it's not necessary, it's good that we have only 8 months. Not quite that, but I know you perfect.

Angry, you buying lace underwear? Silly girl, of course not. Dearie, I don't object as you are the one who is going to wear them, but do get some flannels as I think you must have something thick to have when the cold weather comes and as my future wife, I hope you will take this as you ought to if you know how worried I'll be and also how worried I am for you my little own darling.

How nice of your father to give you the furs you wanted. Must be charming.

I won't mail this letter before I've get the picture which I get at 5.30PM this afternoon. If I cannot write a letter tomorrow, please excuse me, but I'll try. I wish I could. But in the forest there are no post offices. But this long letter will do for two days, won't it min lilla rara älskling (my sweet little darling).

I'll now go and look at rugs, and the lace on the bed sheets and will close and finish up this note when I've got the pictures.

You know, Lina the cook, she has been so kind, she has preserved for our home Dear, such a lot of nice sweet things as strawberries, blackberries, pickled cucumbers and some other nice things. It's watering in my mouth when I write about all these sweet things. Has it any effect on you? No, you are so sweet already so I guess you need nothing extra or do you like all sorts of sweets?

My friends telephoned a second ago that we can't leave for shooting until tomorrow morning at 7AM so I'll stay in town this night too.

Perhaps you've got quite enough of my letter but will just finish it up when I come home.

I have now been and looked at more than one carpet and Dearie, it's very difficult to choose among thousands of carpets and I really found some very nice but they want to know the size we want and the colour of the wallpaper. They will then send home some of them to our flat and I hope my little Olga will like what I have chosen.

I've also been in the shop where the sheets are ordered. Very sorry to say my dear, they are already cut and can hardly be altered.

Dearie, the time, the one and a half months seem like years and our separation so far like a long long time. But dear, I can see you quite as I've seen you during the lucky time in Paris and at Särö, even when we quarrelled, but no more quarrels between you and me. Never, n'est-ce pas?

Darling, excuse my writing, spelling and everything but if I shall write after my thoughts, what my heart feels and after my disposition, then I cannot write slowly and interrupt myself every 10 words. I can't do it the whole time or you will have very short letters. Darling, I'll try to improve myself, min kära Olga.

I just got the photos. You will probably say "You have not combed your hair as I want it", but Dearie, since you left me I've had my hair cut once and when I took the photo, I had wet my hair with water. If you don't like it, tell me straight away and I'll take another one, but I find the one with the right side toward you, very good.

How is your mother and father, Una and Willie -- hope all right.

Dearie, thousands of kisses from your own loving little "baby" Folke

PS: The valise, something like this (enclosed a clipping from a magazine) with about the same fitting. Hope you can find one like this. That's if your father can afford that this year.

Kisses again and good night älskling (darling) Folke

ALMOST BACK TO WORK

August 18, 1909

The strike is still on. This national strike of 1909 was a big loss for the Swedish workers who really had not planned it at all, but were forced into it through the "lockout" by their employers. They eventually had to accept a cut in pay as their unions were weak and did not have the funds to hold out for a long time. The unions received financial help from abroad, but it was not enough.

So when Folke reports that the strike was still on but that the workers, mostly the married men, had begun to return to work, it reflected the economic reality -- they had to go back to work to make a living. There was no other money coming in.

I suppose the reader has already noted the sharp contrast between the well-to-do Olga and Folke furnishing their fine flat in Gothenburg and the bride-to-be, buying furs and lace lingerie in Germany for her trousseau and the poor striking workers going without food. But this was 1909, amidst the remnants of the worst excesses of the "Gilded Age" when the rich were exceedingly rich and the poor exceedingly poor.

Things changed after WW1 and WW2 and the condition of workers became better, culminating in the 1960's. Oddly, since then, the situation for workers has worsened. Globalization and other conditions have brought back the "Gilded Age" and that is where we are today. But we digress. Back to our lovebirds, Folke and Olga and their plans to get married in August of 1909.

In Gothenburg Sweden, at the desk of Folke Jonsson at his father's company where the workers have just gone back to work, we find young and handsome Folke carefully dipping his pen in ink and writing one of his excellent, beautifully executed daily letters to his beloved Olga in Germany. The envelope will be forwarded from Cologne to Wiesbaden, the next stop for the Dawson family on their journey through Europe. The journey will end in Brussels in September and culminate, a month later, in the wedding in Paris of the eighteen year old American Olga Mims Dawson and the twenty-three year old Swedish Folke Jonsson.

```
August 18, 1909
Dearest, Dearest Mimsie,
Thanks very much for your card from Meissen,
min lilla älskling (my little darling).
   I hope you will soon be in Cologne or you
won't hear very much from me (Folke had sent his
last letter to Cologne).
   Darling, I feel like another person after
yesterdays shooting.
   Darling, today our workmen commenced to work
again and I have been out and looked to the
mill. The strike is still bad, but in different
branches the married men are going back to
work more or less. We have nearly everyone back
except 10 men.
   My two English cousins came up today and
visited me in the office. I had dinner together
with them and saw them off at the station.
   Darling, I'm longing so after you, yes I'm so
ledsen (sad) that the time pass so slowly.
   Darling, I'm your true loving baby and you
```

are everything for me.

Dear, when I think of the one and a half months left I nearly burst out crying. I'm longing more and more every day.

Dear I've no time as a lot of work and Papa wants me to come to Särö at 5.25PM.

Good buy for now my little älskling (darling).

Love to all, but everything for you and the very best I can find. I'm always your own true loving, longing "baby" Folke

AUGUST 19, 1909

Olga has asked Folke if he allows others to read her letters and he adamantly declares that he does not. There is still a discussion when exactly the wedding will take place and it now seems that it will be October 17.

The strike is still on in Sweden and the artillery has been called in to clear some streets the day before.

August 19, 1909
My Dearest own Olga,
Thanks very very much for your kind sweet letter and no need to tell you that I read it over and over again.

I could understand you want to put the marriage to the end of October but älskling (darling) why? So Dear, I must thank you that you fixed the date, but you cannot mean the 17th as it is a Sunday. Did you mean that or perhaps I read your figures wrong?

Dearie, I've NOT read any of your letters to either my father or anybody else, but why do you ask me that?

Dearie, why did you say the 7th the other day and now you say the 17th? Dearie, I've to count two months again. I'm longing so after you my Darling.

Yesterday Philip (Krafft) came and had supper with father and me and today we had dinner here together. Papa is well but stayed out at Särö today.

Your picture is in front of me and I smile every time I look at it. I <u>cannot</u> be happy without you. I would take the train and go and see you if I had the time but darling I must work as there is lots to do now as the mill started.

I'm nearly mad of longing so after you but it strengthens my love more and more for every day Älskling (Darling).

Hope you received the long letter and the picture.

You've made me think so much of the "end of October" as you put it. Darling, answer me truthfully what you mean.

Glad to hear that you have got your trousseau as you like it.

Darling, write and answer me plainly on my question and don't think I'm angry or ledsen (sad). I'll wait the extra 10 days with pleasure as you must know "you never wait to long for the best in the world".

Good buy for now Darling. I'm always yours own true loving, longing "baby" Folke

PS. The strike still going on and yesterday the artillery troops cleared some street outside Gothenburg. Otherwise nothing.

Excuse me but I'm in haste as I must catch the train. I would give much for 10 minutes with you just now.

Your ever the same

August 20, 1909

Olga has written to say how much she enjoyed Dresden.

Folke writes that he is looking forward to

October "as a man and the pleasure will double". He asks Olga if she doesn't look forward at all. This is of course code for what he looks forward to -- the sex once they are married. But Olga did not even know how children were made and felt very insecure.

August 20, 1909
Dearest, Dearest Mimsie,
Have no letter today, but dear I hope you are quite well. Also that you are enjoying yourself. Glad to hear you loved Dresden so much, but Dearie, I'm really very jealous.

Dearie, without you there isn't very much which can make me shine up. Not even a cigarette can make me good as I thought and as specially you thought. How could you think Dear, as you thought once, that I loved a cigarette more than you? No, dear, a little thing which goes to ashes in some minutes, but you, living and living.

Dear, I'm so lonely, but I'm really trying to enjoy myself but impossible when you are not with me. I soon hope to be with you but time passes so slowly. Everything I do seems so silly to me without you and I feel I've no heart, it's with you and Dearie, I know I've your heart and that's the only thing making me happy. I take the days as they come, but Dearie, what a difference it would be with you by my side.

My work is very interesting but would not be worth very much if I hadn't you "min kära lilla Olga" (my dear little Olga). I'm sitting quite alone in my father's room (and probably having a drink too because your English is not the best tonight, dear grandfather Folke!) talking with you, all this nonsense, you would say, but Dear, it's true, true as gold. I'm so ledsen (sad), the days are so long.

Darling, I cannot possibly write all I feel for you. Dearie, you must read between the lines.

Älskling (Darling), your letters are for you alone and don't read them to your father or mother. I've never read or let anybody read your letters. I've them locked down and nobody can read them.

Dearie I've fixed that I'll go out shooting tomorrow, Saturday at 3PM and stay out all Sunday. Fromell will come also and he is probably going to buy Lasse's part in the grounds we have.

Darling, I saw you everywhere I looked when I was out shooting last time and that's probably why the birds wouldn't fall for my gun.

Darling, the "teasing card" (the anti smoking postcard with a skull) was splendid. Wouldn't that be nice to have some prints in our smoking room.

Dearie, nothing done in our flat yet, but they will work hard when the strike is over.

I'm looking for a small china vase (for Olga's collection of vases) from Gothenburg, but haven't yet found the shop. Darling, I'm looking forward to October (not too late in the month Dear) as a man and the pleasure will double. Don't you look forward at all?

Love to all. Dearie, I'm always your own true loving, longing
Folke

Will stop in town and here's a kiss xxx from your "little baby".

AUGUST 23, 1909

Finally the workers have started in the flat. Folke reports that he has bought a stove for the hall which means that he will get use for the wood he has bought. They will have to keep their flat warm by burning wood.

Folke's letters are now of more "normal" length.

Work has started and he has work to do at the office where he prefers to write his letters to Olga.

August 23, 1909
Dearest Mimsie,
Thanks awfully much again for your kind sweet letter I received yesterday night when I arrived home to my father's flat. I wrote you a postcard, hope you got it as I asked Fromell to mail it.

We succeeded a little better with the shooting this time as we brought home one hare, three ducks, two black-cocks and also shot one "hobby" or what do you call them, perhaps lark hawk. I'm going to have that bird stuffed by a man at the museum.

Dearie, I've seen the man who rents the flat, our flat, and he told me that the door between the bedroom and the room next to it is ready now and tomorrow they will start putting up the wallpaper and paint.

I've been and bought a stove for the hall, that's all that has been done to our flat. It will be ready the first days of September.

This morning my brother came home from England with a friend and we had breakfast at the Palace. I'm now going out to Särö and have dinner with them. Have some work to do.

Love to all, min lilla älskling "my little darling". Kisses to you, my own darling and I believe me, I'm always <u>your</u> own, true loving ever
  Folke

AUGUST 25, 1909

Time passes slowly for Folke who wishes it would be October. He could have taken a train to be with Olga for a week, had it not been for the work at the office. He reports that he keeps to his promise to keep his smoking down.

August 25, 1909
Dearest, Dearest my own Mimsie,
I can't work, no I can't Dearie, you are too much in my thoughts, I mean never _too_ much, but I'm thinking and wondering how you are. Dearie, my hopes to have a letter on my desk was not completed but I still have the afternoon mail.

Dearie, I went yesterday with my brother an his friend Mr. Hertzig, to a charity afternoon at Särö for the bath women. Nothing extraordinary but very nice and sweet.

Dearie, I can't have any pleasure here without you my Dear. Was it not for the work in the office, nothing could prevent me going down and see you for a week min lilla älskling (my little darling).

Have just finished my dinner and got your letter and must thank you awfully much for it. You can understand Dearie, how much I enjoyed it.

About smoking, I told you in a letter some time ago that I should try to be able to inform you that I hadn't smoked for some time, but that day hasn't yet come, as I wished. But one thing Dear, I have not gone above the _three_. How could you think I should care so little about my promise to _you_.

Dearie, I've no great pleasure going out playing bridge but I suppose when I've promised, I have to go. If I could change the whole afternoon for half a second with you, I wouldn't hesitate. Dearie, I wish we were in October.

Thanks, lilla älskling (little darling) for your postcard, You must be having a glorious time. Dearie, to hear from you is the best pleasure.

Kisses in lots and take the little flower I picked, kissed for you.

Dearie, I'm always your own true baby, ever, your Folke
      Regards in lots and love to all

AUGUST 26, 1909

Folke's friends mock him for not drinking alcohol after his engagement and also for cutting back on smoking, but Folke remains steadfast in his promise to his Olga. As previously said, those who knew Folke as an older man, loving the good life, eating, smoking and drinking, must be very surprised at his resolve, but again, he probably would have done anything for Olga.

August 26, 1909
Dearest my "lilla älskling" (little darling),
Thanks enormous for your letter with the picture with the ruined man you sent me. It's really marvellous to get that card just when I had a dispute with my friends yesterday evening about smoking and also drinking.

Dearie, if you don't believe me, don't believe me, but I <u>always</u> tell you the truth. My three friends all took water (alcohol) for supper, not one but three glasses each. I refused, but they laughed, also when we had our coffee they took brandy after, but I was alright without.

They couldn't understand that when I had liked to take alcohol before I got engaged to you my Darling, I've stopped it now. They are so silly not understanding. <u>I</u> know you don't like me to take it.

Nothing could persuade me doing something I know you don't like. Also about smoking, they made fun of me but I only smiled and said "I don't care".

Above the three (cigarettes a day) I will never go without your permission.

I had a very nice bridge game last night and won 1,8 kronor but could have won much more if I hadn't played so bad, so they told me, but I don't know.

Dearie, I'm so busy as Mr. Lundberg is going away on his wedding trip on Wednesday. I think

I have to take all his work, but it's all right, that makes the time pass quicker until the 18th of October. I have to work all day long, so no time to go out to Särö, I'm quite sure.

Dearie, please write me by return of post, if 1891 was the right year and the 10th of January.

I'm longing to meet again darling. I wish I could fly.

Everybody tells me that I'm not here, I must be somewhere else. I know where I am.

Can you guess, I forgot to tell you I played tennis the day before yesterday with Philip and afterwards we talked with Dagmar. She asked me if I didn't feel funny to marry so soon and various questions.

I think you see too many nice men out on your trip. Take care of your heart. It's mine I hope just as much as you have mine. N'est-ce pas?

My brother Axel is turning up at the villa at Särö, and we are going to have a supper for his friends on Saturday I think. I'm not very much for those suppers, I don't enjoy them when I know I have my little älskling far away in Germany.

Dearie, I think our flat is ready the first of September, with new paper on the walls, and new paint afterwards. I can begin to see the flat and will have it ready by the time I leave for Paris about the 10th of October.

Love to Una, your father, mother and Willie.

Dearie, I'll write you every day about the cigarettes. Yesterday a little cigar and one cigarette, that's all.

I'm trying to stop altogether and today up to 11AM, no smoking.

Well Dearie, I have work to do so I must close with love from your own longing true ever your "baby"

Folke

August 27, 1909

Folke has to do two men's work when his co-worker Mr. Lundberg is on his honeymoon. He still writes his daily letter to Olga, but they are considerably shorter, nothing like the thirty-six page letter he wrote while the strike continued earlier that month. He always wrote after work, at the office. In another letter he wrote that the best place to write letters, was in the office because there was always good paper and ink there.

Olga's father has asked for a letter from a bank that Folke has forwarded. probably some sort of statement about Folke's financial situation.

August 27, 1909
My own Dearest Darling,
Dearie, I feel I must have a little talk with you now when daywork is finished. Lots of work but I have always time to write to you, even if I havn't any time. I should make time.

Dearie, after having written you yesterday, I had dejeuner with my brother and cousin Sandberg, also Philip (Krafft) and Axel's friend Philip, stood the whole thing and when I drank the champagne I thought of you min lilla älskling (my little darling). For dessert we got ice cream, I wished you could have had some "Après dinner".

I smoked a cigarette and after dejeuner, another, that's all for yesterday although the other boys offered me the poison many times.

Dearie, we had a good dinner. The others went up to the restaurant in the afternoon but I had no alcohol, only some lemonade.

I've forwarded a letter from your father today from a bank. Hope it's the one you asked for.

Dearie, my thoughts are going to you all the time, I can see you everywhere, I only wish it was in reality.

Papa gave me some letters to write so will close.

Good buy and think sometimes of your own longing, loving, always your

Folke

AUGUST 28, 1909

Folke's father is having a party for all the young people, 28 in all, at Särö, and as Folke often does when he writes about a party, says that there will be "ice cream". That seems like nothing special to us, but in those days, it was a luxury. When electric refrigerators and freezers did not exist, the ice cream would have to be prepared just before the dessert in a machine where ice pieces (taken from an ice storage where ice collected in the winter was stored all year along under thick layers of sawdust) would be put into a machine with salt and then wound with a large handle for a very long time. The salt made the ice colder and after a lot of cranking a delicious ice cream was ready to be eaten right away.

August 28, 1909
Miss Olga M. Dawson
c/o Thos Cook Son
KÖLN (Cologne)
Germany

My own Dearest Mimsie,

Dearie, only a few words to let you know how I am. Quite well, hope the same and also that I may have a letter from you min lilla älskling.

Smoked one cigarette after dinner and one after supper. Is it too many?

We are going to have a party tonight for all the young people at Särö. All nice good things, ice cream etc. Wish of all my heart you could be with me but you are not with me.

In all we will be 28 persons. Dearie, will

write you more about it tomorrow.

Darling, Papa and I will come to Paris about a week before the 18th (October), how I'm longing to see you and talk with you, älskling. These parties I don't like when you aren't here.

Dearie, must help my father now. Hope to hear from you tomorrow.

I'm always your own own loving, longing "baby"
Folke

Excuse in haste.

AUGUST 29, 1909

It is Sunday, but Folke is in the office because he wants to check for letters from Olga. On Sunday? People worked on Saturdays in those days, but of course had Sunday off, but it seems that there were mail deliveries, at least to companies such as Jonsson, Sternhagen & Co. Folke is disappointed since he has not heard from Olga for three days!

Folke tells Olga about the party the day before, a typical Swedish August crayfish party. He doesn't drink anything and tries to stop smoking, and how he longs for his Olga!

August 29, 1909
My Dearest own Olga,
It's Sunday today and I've come to town to see if there are any letters from you. No, there were no letters, not a single word. Haven't heard from you in three whole days.

Well my Darling, it's only 6PM so I've time to spare with you.

Dearie, we had that party yesterday night, rather nice but you can understand that I couldn't enjoy it very much Darling.

The garden was decorated with Chinese lanterns and we had fireworks also in the garden. It's unnecessary to write all the names of the young people as all young ones were there of our age.

We had ice cream, lots of crayfish and chicken

but when I had the ice cream I was thinking about Paris and our first tea in Bois de Bologne, we had ice cream afterwards. Dearie, if it's open when I come to Paris, we must go to all the nice places and see if they are alike.

Dearie, I'm longing so after you that I am nearly crying, not far off.

Dearie, I've ordered the picture you want and will send them as soon as I get them. Another thing, I've taken a picture today with my panama on, would you like to see it, when ready?

We danced yesterday after supper and would you believe it, I danced too. With Dagmar, the black girl and a few others. After the dance, we all, I mean only the men went to the restaurant. I had a lemonade Dearie, and when finished I went home and left all the other still drinking.

During the day yesterday I smoked a pipe and one cigarette and no more today. I think smoking a pipe sometimes is better than cigarettes.

Dearie, I feel very lonely, yes Dearie, I love you so much and I'm true as gold to you. You've got my heart, yes indeed, the whole big heart. Älskar du mig? (Do you love me?)

Dearie, I pray tonight that I will soon hear from you, I'm longing for a letter. You are always in my prayers, the last thing before I go to bed.

Dearie, I'm your own loving, longing ever your "baby" Folke

Love to your father, mother and Una and Willie.

The best for you xxxx and good night

AUGUST 30, 1909

Finally a letter from Olga and Folke's spirits are up. He is concerned about Olga's birth certificate which she cannot obtain since she was born in Kingston New Mexico 1891 during a "Silver Rush "when there were no proper registration of births in this frontier town. The silver was far more interesting than keeping records of births. It was from growing up here that Olga had memories of an Indian attack and being rolled up in mattresses to escape the their arrows. When her family left for New York, the stage coach was attacked by bandits and Olga's grandmother was frightened and dropped Olga's baby sister who later died.

Though Folke is doing two men's work at the office, he manages to write to Olga, this time from his father's flat where has talked to the servant "Fina" who is trying to find the best servants for Olga and Folke. I can imagine that she would have been very fond of the kind and handsome "Mr. Folke" as she calls him.

The strike is still on but most workers are back at work. Folke tells Olga that their saw mill has new machinery, some of the most modern in the business.

August 30, 1909
My own Dearest,
How happy I am having received your letter, the one telling me that you, my little darling, was going to Cologne the same day. I can quite understand that you all are having a delightful time just travelling about from place to place.

Dearie, that's a good girl having written for the papers, but Dearie, try to find a way to get the birth papers, or if you can't get them, ask the consulate what you are going to do without them.

Please write me a few lines when you've received the other papers so we have them in order because without the necessary papers, we cannot marry.

Dearie, today I have taken all the work of Mr. Lundberg on my shoulders as he is too busy to attend to any work now when he will marry on Wednesday this week. He is going on his wedding trip Copenhagen-Dresden-Vienna-Venice-Milano and to see all the Italian lakes and back home through Germany. Hope they will have fine weather.

Yes Dearie, Miss Carlsson (Axeline) has left us and is now in Marstrand. I miss her but she will soon come in to town and will then be of great help to me as she has promised to help us with the flat. I've moved my things or rather, have had my things sent in today from Särö as I must be all day long in the office and work hard.

Dearie, the time was passing away slowly yesterday after having finished your letter, yes would you believe my own Darling, I went to bed at 8PM and father came home just about the same time and said that I was mad or something like it.

Good sleep and fresh air makes a world of good, that's perfectly true Dearie. The time is passing and I'm now counting the weeks till I can pack my trunk and go off to Paris. Well I count about five weeks!!

Dearie, do you object to marry at the Swedish legation as I wrote you sometime ago? That's the easiest way and not at the "Palais de Justice".

I'm now going to have my little dinner "tout seule" (all alone) in my father's flat. Why can't you be with me? Guess not, too far away, but soon you will be here and then no more "tout seule". Will finish this note when I've finished dinner.

Just finished dinner quite alone and during the whole time I was discussing the servant matters with our old one, "Fina". Do you remember? Dearie, she is running all over town to try to get the very best servants she can get as she wants Mr. Folke to have good servants, one looking after the home and one who can give us good food and keep the house clean.

Dearie, when I think of us settled in our

flat, I nearly cry of happiness. Thanks Darling for your nice sweet postcard from Coblenz, you must have a glorious time.

Dearie, nothing new about the strike, we are personally not harmed by it now as we have nearly our mill quite as usual. Only a few workmen are missing. I'm there nearly every day and it is very interesting. All the new machinery work beautifully and I think we've got one of the most modern mills in our line of business.

Dearie I kept my promise I made in my letter yesterday, not to smoke any more yesterday night and I did keep it. Haven't smoked a single cigarette today, only a pipe. A pipe more today probably, no cigarette as it is a poison. Don't you think so Dearie? I guess you do.

Give your dear father and mother, Una and Willie my very best regards and love. Will be tickled to death to see you all again. And you Dearie for ever, yes indeed for ever. Darling, I'm longing more and more after you

Please ask about the birth certificate Dearie. My love to you älskling (darling) and my very best prayers you will be doing well. I am your own, always your "baby" Folke

EMBROIDERY FOR OLGA

AUGUST 31, 1909

Folke is worried that Olga and her family will go to Holland where there has been a cholera outbreak.

Folke has been to see the new flat and he and his father have bought carpets for it. Folke has also started embroidering something for Olga. It will be a surprise.

August 31, 1909
My own Dearest Mimsie,
Thanks very, very much for your sweet letter I received this morning when I came to my office. Dearie, you should see how happy I get to receive <u>your</u> letters. How can you think I'm too much occupied to have time to read your letters, of course not. Still I have a lot of work now. I'm not so busy Dearie. I'm so glad to hear you are asking for information about the marriage as we must have everything in order and we haven't got so very much time left. Jolly glad we haven't.

Dearie, do be careful in Holland for the cholera as I've been reading in the papers that many people have been dying from it. Why go to Brussels. Leave direct for Paris from Cologne. Then you need not risk anything. I only say this as I'm so afraid that something shall happen to you and your family. Don't drink plain ordinary water. Dearie, be careful, if not for anything else, but for <u>me.</u>

Have just come back to the office after having had my dinner at a friend's home. After that we visited our flat and the papering is ready in the bedroom, my toilette room, and the extra servant room. It looks grand Dearie, and Papa and I have just been and bought the carpets. He is simply darling and I hope you will like them.

Dearie, everything has to be made without you, but I'm certain that I have followed your taste.

I'm again alone in the office and the best time I can spend is when I'm writing to you Dearie. It's almost perfect to think that we have come so far now, only one month until I can begin to pack my things.

I'm going to start embroidering something for you, but I'm not going to tell you what it is, you will see it when I come back with you to our own flat. Now, have I made you curious? N'est-ce pas? Dearie, you like surprises, don't you?

Smoked 2 pipes yesterday, no cigarettes yesterday and today. Good boy, isn't he?

Dearie, write me about the marriage as soon as possible.

Love to all and the best for you "älskling" (darling).

I'm always your own loving longing ever your "baby", true as gold,
Folke

SEPTEMBER 1, 1909

This is a short letter because Folke is now alone at the office and he also wants to please his father by going out to Särö. He reminds Olga that he spent the evening embroidering. It will come as a surprise to many relatives and friends of Folke that he as a young man, eagerly waiting to marry Olga, embroidered something for his Olga. Very endearing.

September 1, 1909
My Dearest Olga,
Thanks very much Dear for your sweet postcard, kära (dear) Mimsie.

  Very busy but will rush on a few lines to you. I couldn't be myself if I hadn't talked a little with you darling. I'm longing so after you and I spent the whole evening after office time with embroidering

  Papa gone out to Särö, he wants me to come out to him, but I'm not quite sure he will have me there as a lot of work and besides Mr. Lundberg was married today and left the office for a month. Yes, my time will come next to leave the office and come down to see you Dearie.

  Darling I must close now as I'll try to make Papa happy and go out to the little Särö, full of nice sweet remembrances.

  Give my love to everybody and believe me Dearie, I've not smoked any more cigarettes since Sunday, just a pipe or two.

  I'm always your own true loving "baby". There's some sweet xxx xxx xxx for you älskling (darling), Ever your own Folke

SEPTEMBER 2, 1909

Folke again warns Olga against going to Holland where cholera has recently been reported in the papers. He wouldn't want anything to happen to his beloved.

  It seems that Olga and Folke have a leather sofa and chairs for their flat -- probably bought when Olga was in Sweden over the summer. Folke has now bought a matching writing chair and ordered curtains.

  Folke's mother Ragnhild was artistic and had gone to art school. Folke may have got his creative side from her. Olga and Folke knew each other well and had Olga not been convinced that Folke would make good choices, she would have insisted on doing all the purchases together. She probably loved the idea of Folke happily buying furnishings for the flat and working on an embroidery surprise for her in the evenings. He certainly does not sound like the average young man about to be married. He has reduced his smoking and he does not touch alcohol, all because of his promise to Olga.

September 2, 1909
My own darling Mimsie,
Dearie, thanks very much for your postcard from Cologne. Very glad to know that you have safely reached that town. I've only travelled through the station two or three times.

Dearie, I'm surprised that you are going to Brussells and Holland when you can read in the papers that the cholera is going more and more there. Guess now it's impossible to alter, but Dearie, be <u>careful</u>.

I'm longing so after you Dearie, I think of you even when I'm quite full of work.

I succeeded in going to Särö yesterday. Papa had invited Mr. and Mrs. Blidberg for bridge and we played on till a thunderstorm began when the lady got afraid and was anxious to go home to her children.

I've been to the furniture shop and bought a chair for our writing desk, lined with the same leather as the sofa and chairs. I'm going this afternoon to decide about the curtains. I don't like to have everything done in a rush, so I order everything slowly.

Yes Dearie, I have not smoked any cigarettes yet and I'm lightning a pipe and it lasts me a long time.

Kära Olga (Dear Olga), love to all. The very best I have got for you my true heart and xxxx xxxx from your own always longing, loving "baby" Folke

SEPTEMBER 3, 1909

Folke has a lot to do at the office and receives news about a collision which affects one of the steamers belonging to the company.

Folke still has not had Olga's confirmation of the year she was born so he asks once more. He had not anticipated how hard it would be to do two men's work, but seems determined to make a go of it.

Folke refers to some Daily Mail articles that Olga had mentioned. There was a series of articles on "early marriage" and Olga had closely followed the debate. Many preferred early marriages at the time and our young couple belonged to those who wanted to be married early.

It is interesting to know what Folke did in the office: writing letters, invoices and Bills of Ladings. And at the end of the day, of course, a letter for Olga (in Brussels).

```
September 3, 1909
My own Dearest Mimsie,
Dearie, thanks for your long sweet letter from
Cologne. Thanks again.
   Dearie, the time is past six and I've just
finished work, yes indeed I've been in hard work
the whole long day, not a minute free more than
for dinner which I had quite alone. Hope it
won't be many more dinners I shall have to take
alone.
   No Dearie, you needn't fear that I shall go
or have gone above the three!!!! (cigarettes).
I love you too much to do that, same goes for
alcohol. Never.
   Dearie, that's not a bother to marry in Paris.
If you only get the necessary papers, it will
work as well as at any other place.
   I just got the unfortunate news that a man
of war (Australian) visiting Gothenburg, had
collided with one of our steamers just a few
minutes from here in the river and the machinery
```

room is filled with water and has to go to land. Such trouble! We will probably have to go out in a tug and see that the steamer will be landed all right. Enough of this, but I'll write you tomorrow what had happened to the boat. We will not loose any money as it was the Australian steamer which ran over ours.

I bought the curtains yesterday, just the ones you liked and I'm so glad that's done.

Dearie, you've not written me if 1891 was the correct year of your birth. Then you're only eighteen years, and nineteen, next January. Is that so?? Please write me as it is important to get my papers ready.

I didn't know it was so much work to do without Mr. Lundberg. I can and will manage it.

I've not read the Daily Mail articles, but translations have turned up in the last Swedish newspapers. It seems that early marriages are preferred. N'est-ce pas?

Dearie, I beg you to be careful with the cholera in Holland!!

Dearie, you've been writing the whole day and so have I, yes at least about forty letters, invoices besides a lot of Bill of Ladings. You must excuse my handwriting but I do let the pen slide like it likes, or like my heart wants.

It's so calm here in the office, not a word and I'm quite alone, not alone Dear, I've your picture in front of me and you are always in my heart.

I haven't smoked any cigarettes yet, only the pipe when I light it a second or two, but it won't keep lighted and I don't care to light it again.

Dearie, I wish I was ready to go to Paris. You don't write me about your trousseau. Have you bought any new nice things? Guess loads. I'm ledsen (sad), not ledsen Dearie, only longing so after you.

My embroidering is going on fine. I's something for you, I mean for our bedroom.

Guess you must think this quite enough rots, excuse me, don't know if you can write a word like that to <u>a lady</u>. Well Dearie, good night and I'm always your own longing ever your "baby" Folke
Love to all

SEPTEMBER 4, 1909

Folke is still concerned about Olga going to Holland because of the cholera there. In an earlier letter Olga mentioned that it would be fun to go to Holland and "live a peasant's life", probably some sentimental scheme concocted by a travel agent. It must have caught young Olga's imagination and she mentioned the idea of it in a letter to Folke. She never went to Holland, but she had Folke very worried.

Folke reports that the strike will be over on Monday, (September 6) but that 6,000 men will be out of work as they have been "declared in lock out". This was a disastrous strike for many workers who had to leave Sweden and go to America to find jobs as their employers did not wish them back. I think that Folke and his father were fair minded employers, treated their workers well and did not cause them unnecessary hardship.

The matter of the collision with the company steamer has been settled as the culprit, an Argentinian (not Australian) vessel was not allowed to leave until they paid for the repairs.

September 4, 1909
Dearest Dearest,
I received your letter and postcard this morning, the letter containing some pictures of chandeliers and the postcard the map of your trip. Dearie, you must enjoy such a trip. Think of it simply as travel from town to town

and see different places, different people and talk different languages. The only thing I would object to if I could, was that you're going to Holland to live a peasant's life.

I cannot do anything about it, but my prayers when going to sleep is that nothing shall happen to you, älskling (darling). Delightful to make or rather do something like that, but not when people are dying like flies of cholera.

Dearie, when do you expect to be in Paris?

I really find the chandelier very nice and Dear, why not get one like it for the hall? Can you give me the name and address of the firm so I could write and order the catalogue and also about the table for tea. I like it very much, is it the same address?

Darling, after having mailed your letter yesterday I worked a little bit more and answered in the telephone, all the inquiries about the collision and went down to the station and and had a talk with Fritz Sternhagen, and then home at 9PM to have my supper. Tout seule (All alone).

Dearie, it is now Saturday again and Dearie, and I'm quite alone again at the office talking with you. Papa gone out to Särö as he was invited to Mr. Lindström for dinner and a bridge party. I'll probably go out shooting tomorrow if the weather will be better, but no pleasure when it's raining the whole long day.

The strike will be finished on Monday and part of the workmen will go back to work, but about 6,000 men in Gothenburg will be out of work as they are declared in lock out.

Dearie, I'm so glad you are quite well, "touch wood" but don't be afraid that I will overwork myself. No, I'm strong enough to take on more work. My only sickness is that I'm longing so for you Dear, hope soon to be by your side.

Dearie, which do you prefer, to have the telephone in the hall or in the smoking room?

In the hall, we can place the phone on a rack, but in the smoking room, on the desk. Where to put the furniture in that room? Like this (sketch supplied)?

Do you like it like the drawing or do you want it anywhere else? I must know, I have to give the telephone men order where to put in the wires.

I've not smoked a cigarette in one whole week. I'm rather proud of myself, but it is for you Dearie, only for you and smoking is poison.

Dearie, I'm thinking of you every second that passes, think, those seconds will never come back and I'm not with you, what a waste of time of our lives.

Dearie, how lovely it will be with all the vases on the sideboard in our dining room. Dearie, don't worry if it's bad weather on our honeymoon, we will have fine weather. Our love will warm up the air and we won't feel the cold. Don't worry min lilla älskling (my little darling).

The boat, man of war, that our steamer collided with yesterday, was Argentinian, not Australian. It is not allowed to leave until the matter is settled. We are insured, so no loss.

Ta, Ta, min kära Mimsie (my dear Mimsie). Hope to hear from you tomorrow. Love to all from your own loving true "baby"
Ever Folke

SEPTEMBER 5, 1909

Folke writes one of his shorter letters to Olga. He likes his daily chat with her and to keep her informed of what goes on. So far he has written Olga a letter every single day since they parted in Malmö at the beginning of August. Tomorrow he will deal with household plans.

September 5, 1909
Dearest my own Mimsie,
 Think Dearie, I'm again in the office, it's Sunday and I just came in from Särö with Papa. We took a walk around the villas at Särö and I felt so lonely as we visited the tall boys mother, but she wasn't at home. Only the fiancée. Darling, I wish the time would pass away quicker.
 Dearie, tomorrow I'll decide about the servants. Will write you as soon as anything is done.
 Went to the moving pictures yesterday and after, an hour embroidering and at 10PM, to bed.
 Haven't smoked more than a pipe. Dearie, Papa wants me to leave now, so good bye and sleep well. He sends his love to all. So do I also of course.
 Darling, I'm longing so after you älskling. I'm always your own ever loving, longing "baby" true for ever your Folke.

SEPTEMBER 6, 1909

Folke is blown away by Olga's suggestion that they postpone the wedding for three months to have more time to think about it. Could he not go on a few months longer without her she asks? She has written that she is nervous and asks Folke if he isn't nervous too. She is more afraid than happy, she wrote, so obviously something was bothering her. *"Would you like to postpone the whole affair until spring??? I'm willing if you are".*

Olga was eighteen years old and about to be married, but no one had told her The Facts of Life. That came later, as a surprise. My mother explained to me that her mother Olga thought she would become pregnant when her husband Folke touched her on her leg, but one never knows precisely what went on in young Olga's mind. She had written to Folke on more than one occasion that there was something she wanted to talk to him about, face to face, before the ceremony and now she brings up the idea of postponing the wedding.

My grandmother who in later life, always appeared unafraid and superbly confident, did indeed have something on her mind. She was after all still a teenager and her brain must have been bursting. She proceeded with the wedding as planned, but nevertheless did ask Folke if they should not delay it. This was no doubt a natural reaction when one marries so young.

Perhaps Olga was simply testing Folke to discover what he really felt. Had they been together, Folke might have reassured her and put her at ease. He was certainly most loving and expressed this love in a letter every day. One day in Germany, when Olga arrived at a new destination, she had four letters waiting for her and she received another two letters later that same day. Could one wish for a more devoted fiancée? If Olga was testing Folke, she finds out that a postponement would "kill him" and he asks her not to bring it up again.

Folke agrees with Olga to keep the wedding simple. Folke must again ask about Olga's birth date. He has not had her definite answer yet. And Olga will soon be going to Paris to attend to papers they need.

```
September 6, 1909
My Dearest Olga,
```
   Thank you so much for your sweet letter Dear and I cannot understand it. Thanks for the consulate letter and I'm glad you won't have any troubles with your papers. I'm sending back the letter in case you want same.
   Dearie, you know very well how I'm longing for October and now Dearie when everything is

nearly at the end you ask me if I would like to postpone the whole thing for three months. I cannot answer you anything on that, only you know me to well to expect an answer.

Dearie, you've got me in your hands and I didn't think I could insist upon you. Could you propose to me what I should do the whole three months? Darling, it would be the same as killing me. No Dearie, don't be afraid. It's a whole month and a week still. You don't ask me again, will you Dear????? I can't say I should like to postpone it. Never, not unless you say you don't want to marry.

Darling, thanks for the photos, they are rather good, the one of the whole family.

Visited the flat today and all rooms are papered now. Fine they are Dearie.

I agree to the wedding at the Mayor, that's all right and the simplest I think too. Will write you about the invitations. If I send the names in a day or two, they won't be many and nobody will come that far except my brother the artist (Rolf Jonsson). I think so. Perhaps Lasse Bratt. More about that in a few days.

Dear, how I felt ledsen (sad) when I saw the address in the corner of the envelope "Hotel Empire" (in Brussells). Wished I could be there in the little room and the stairs, my room and everything. I can see everything as if it passed before me yesterday (most likely, this is the hotel where Olga and Folke met).

I love you so much Dearie, do you not feel happy at all? Not a tiny bit, answer me????

Cant you write and tell me if 1891 is the right year of your birth because then you're only 18 ----?????

Darling, write me about everything you're deciding. We've decided the 18th of October for our wedding n'est-ce pas???

Smoked two pipes yesterday.

You'll attend to the papers as soon as you

come to Paris. Write me if you want any papers from me.

I'm cheering up, but I'm nearly crying. Don't you love me so much that you will marry me as decided? Guess yes. Hope so at least. Älskling (Darling), of course you love me. Without you I'm not worth much.

Darling, good bye and love to all.
xxx Kiss from Your own loving, longing always your true loving ever Folke

SEPTEMBER 7, 1909

Folke has been to their flat and he will be able to move in the next Monday. Their telephone number will be 3134. Folke thought those numbers would be easy for his American wife to say in Swedish. Ever the thoughtful husband to be, and what a sweetheart he is who goes home to continue embroidering on his homemade surprise gift for Olga!

September 7, 1909
Dearest Dearest,
I've not received any letter from you today, so I cannot thank you. Never mind, just a few lines to tell you that I visited our flat today and they are busy painting. Will put in the bath tub tomorrow and I can begin and move in on Monday next.

I've also been at the telephone station and ordered a telephone for us and I took the number 3134 quite simply for you to say in Swedish, n'est-ce pas? Do you like that number? It's difficult to decide everything alone. I know your taste pretty well but still...

How are you getting along Älskling (Darling). I went with my friend Ewert yesterday evening to a marathon race here at Gothenburg. Very sporting but rather tiresome. Three hours to see.

Smoked two pipes yesterday and today only

half a pipe. It is 5.30PM so you must know I'm not smoking any cigarettes yet. Älskar dig mycket mera min Kära. (Love you much more my Dear). Will close and go home and embroider. I'll think of you as always the whole time I sow.

Kisses from your own, always your loving, longing "baby" Folke

SEPTEMBER 8, 1909

Folke is worried, he has not heard from Olga since Monday, and it is Wednesday!

He asks when Olga is going to Paris and mentions the "30 days" rule that if you wish to marry in Paris, one of the two of you must have been there for at least 30 days. So Olga must soon go there and register.

He wonders if the painful separation really has been necessary.

September 8, 1909
Dearest,Dearest Mimsie,

Dearie, what's the matter? Haven't heard from you since Monday and it's Wednesday today. Hope you've got my letters. I've written to Brussels Cook every day. When are you coming to Paris? Please inform yourself Dear about the 30 days and if our stay in Paris during winter and spring will count. If not, either you or I have to stay in Paris that time.

Dear, I felt like I had to go and see you today. I'm not far from rushing from the office and down to the railway station to see you Dear. As the days are coming more and more nearer our meeting, I am longing more and more. Oh Dear, I'm going here quite alone and nobody interests me. Only you, min Kära Olga (my Dear Olga)

I really don't know if I'm going out shooting as Papa wants me home, he will be 65 years on Sunday. Think dear, when we will be 65. Don't think too much.

After finishing your letter yesterday, I just went home and continued the embroidery and had supper "tout seule". Had a lovely bath and went to bed.

Dear, today also alone at the dinner table. Folke, you'll have a letter tomorrow, he hopes so at least.

I'll be in Paris I hope the 10th if not a few days earlier. Think, only four weeks and we can go out to Bois de Boulogne and take ice cream. Dear, has this separation been necessary? It's too hard to be separated so long from the one I love so much. Dear, I cannot write any more, if I did, I would cry.

Love to all from your loving, longing always your "baby" The very best for you xxx kisses from your Folke

My thoughts are going back to the train between Brussels-Antwerp, my room, Olga and Folke going in a cafe' -- everything dear.

SEPTEMBER 9, 1909

Folke is concerned that Olga has not written - is she angry, or has she not received his letters?
For his peace of mind, I hope he will get a letter tomorrow!

September 9, 1909
Miss Olga Mims Dawson
c/o Thos Cook & Son
41 Rue de la Madeleine
Bruxelles
Belgium
Min lilla Älskling,
My hopes to get a note from you today has gone to pieces. My work specially today, has gone mechanical. You've been in my thoughts the whole day long, not a minute, not a second of

the time has passed without my brain working out and thinking what has happened to my little own Darling so far away from me.

Haven't heard from you since Monday and it's Thursday now 7.20PM. Just finished my work and can't go to bed without having a little chat with you. Dear, are you angry with me? Why, what have I done? Älskling, will put the full street address on the envelope, perhaps you've not received my letters written every day.

Think Dear, time passes and we are soon near the wedding. Oh, Dearest you'll be the star in our flat, it's so nice up there. Just been there and they had just brought up the bath tub. I visited the flat after dinner.

Darling, I can't write more as my brain is nearly bursting. Let me have a letter tomorrow. Love to all. Lasse (Bratt) sends his love and he will certainly come to Paris to our wedding.

Dearest, good night and you know where you have your own, always loving, longing "baby" Folke

September 10, 1909

It is Friday and Folke is delighted, quite a new man after Olga's letter. It turns out that many of his letters arrived together.

The question of Olga's year of birth is still not settled and Folke asks Olga to telegraph him.

Folke has not smoked any cigarettes for two weeks but he smokes a pipe sporadically.

September 10, 1909
Dearest, Dearest,
Your little "baby" is happy, happy like anything having received a letter from you. Thanks lots Dearie.

Cannot possibly understand that you got the letters in a bunch. I've written them every day and mailed them right away. Well, never mind Dear. I have only been so ledsen (sad) not hearing a word from my little Olga. I'm simply someone else now since I received your letter. Even my work interests me.

Sorry to say I haven't got any letter more than the first saying that you were born 1891. Then you write me today that 1891 was the date of my birth and not 1890, the latter date was written hurriedly.

Excuse me that I cannot make it out which date 1891 or 1890. It is very important for my certificate, that we get the same date for <u>our</u> papers, would you telegraph me only one of the years on Monday on the address "Sternhagen, Gothenburg". That's only three words and we can get this matter settled at once. You see, I must get my certificate finished in time.

Dearie, I'm going out shooting today, simply grand of father to giving me a holiday tomorrow as I have worked so hard this week. Dearie, when I have some hours left during the day, I'm embroidering. It's going on fine.

Will finish the letter when I have worked, and then some minutes for you. No Dear, all minutes are for you and will always be. I'll be back here tomorrow night and will just go to Axvall to Hjalmar and Ruth (Folke's sister) for dinner with Papa as it's his 65th birthday.

You are smiling in the photo in front of me, Dearie take a photo of you just as you are and send me, just a cheap one, little one. Dear, I miss you so much and I'm longing so after you.

Could you send me the address of the store where you saw the lamps and tea table.

No cigarettes as it's not good for Folke and besides as you don't like it. Can't possibly make out why you didn't receive my letters in order.

Don't visit Holland Dear, it's really dangerous.

I send you my own Dearest Olga some good long X-------------- kisses and take care of yourself min lilla Älskling (Darling).

Smoked a quarter of a pipe today. Think, tomorrow, two weeks without cigarettes, not one.
   I'm always your own loving, longing "baby".
Ever Folke
Please send your year of birth by telegram.

SEPTEMBER 11, 1909

Folke has been out in the fresh air on a hunting expedition and reports what he has shot. He will bring partridges to his sister and they will all feast on them for dinner.

September 11, 1909
My Dearest Dearest,
Have just received your letter when I returned from my shooting expedition. Thanks lots, it made me so happy. Dear, have finished supper having had a lovely bath.
   Going up to Axvall tomorrow for the day. Dearie, you have been in my thoughts the whole day long. Not a minute out of my thoughts.
   Dearie, I've spent two lovely days out from from town just "camping" you know, having our meals out in the fields.
   Yesterday we only shot four wild ducks, one hare and today, fourteen partridges. Brought some home and we will bring them to Axvall and have them for dinner tomorrow.
   I also shot another hawk but will not have it stuffed as it isn't a good one. Fromell and Mr. Fiedler, my shooting friend, will have another day of hunting tomorrow, but I've had quite enough today, seven partridges on my part.
   Smoked two pipes yesterday. Dearie, excuse the writing (lead pencil) but no ink in the flat. Will write you on the train tomorrow.
   Love to all. Kisses from your own Folke xxx

SEPTEMBER 13, 1909

Folke has been to his sister's house to celebrate his father's 65th birthday. It was a small family celebration. There is nothing that interests Folke, only Olga's letters. Fortunately, the embroidery has a therapeutic effect.

September 13, 1909
My own Dearest Darling,
I'm now back from my trip to Axvall and my shooting as I told you in the little note I sent the other night.

Had the most glorious weather when out shooting and today and yesterday, the weather was just as fine. Can't believe it's September.

We spent a fine time at Axvall, but rather short as we had to come back to the office you understand. We had quite a nice and very good dinner at the Atterboms together with a friend and his wife, Captain Lieberath. I should have, or rather wanted to mail a line to you älskling (darling) yesterday but we came home too late.

Have now finished my dinner tout seule (completely alone), what do you think about that? Yes, Dearie, when I then continued my embroidery for an hour after dinner, I thought, why couldn't you be with me. I feel lonely the whole day long, yes indeed the whole long time we've been separated. I haven't got a line from you since Saturday. I hope you are doing well and the telegram to my father you sent him, I felt fresh regards also from you.

Dearie, so kind of you all to telegraph him. I think he has written your dear Papa today.

Yes Dear, already the 13th and we are not far from October. Had a letter this afternoon from Cappelen (a friend of theirs). He said he expected you to be in Paris, but not in 10 Rue Chalgrin. He is wrong but he said that he will always help you if we need anything he can do. He is a very good friend.

Smoked just a little cigar yesterday. Do you think I'm awful to continue to smoke?

Do you remember that time in the stairs? You're always with me Dear and I'm longing so after you. Dear, you are certainly tired of all my letters. If you knew how I'm looking for you letters. That's the only thing interesting me, when I can read what my little Mimsie has to say.

I'm sorry too Dear, not having your mother over here, but can't they come over for Xmas? Your Dear mother has always been such a good <u>friend</u> to us. I'll <u>never</u> forget it.

Dear I wished you were here. When work does not occupy me, your work (the embroidery) occupies me. It's nothing very grand and difficult but it takes time and I think it will suit the room.

My brother Axel is now back in London and I hope he will come to the wedding, so also my eldest brother. Tomorrow I'll send you the names for the invitations. I'll first talk the matter over with Papa.

At the dinner, all drank your health and mine and it's so hard to receive such an honour without you.

I'm always your true little loving, longing always the same "baby"

Folke

xxx------xxx-----xxx-----Kisses, long ones to you Älskling

SEPTEMBER 14, 1909

Folke has picked out the material for his travelling suit and sent Olga a sample. She will also order her own. The flat awaits the new couple and Folke dreams of the time that they will spend the evenings together.

There is a mention of a Mrs. Dickson who lost her husband (no details) and after his death gave birth to his child.

September 14, 1909
Dearest, Dearest Mimsie,
Many many thanks for your long sweet letter and also for your telegram Dear. So kind of you and now we know that's settled (the year of Olga's birth).

Oh Dear, I'm really sorry for you and for myself too that your mother, father and Willie are staying in Brussels (as opposed to Paris) but Dearie, it's not far away and we will see them don't you think Darling?

To show you dear what kind of stuff I have ordered for my travelling suit, I enclose a sample of the material. Do you like it? I've taken grey, not to let dust be seen so very much. It is double breasted, square cut. Hope you like it. Also ordered a blue one just alike. Dearie, you've got such a good taste, so you choose what you like (Folke must be speaking of Olga's travel suit) but I think a grey tailor made, would be very good and useful.

I have been to the flat just after dinner, tomorrow I can begin to have carpets put in etc. Dear, do you think we better wait with buying chandeliers and have them put up when we have come home from our wedding trip? Or do you leave it to me? Couldn't you make a drawing what kind you want or something close to it.

I'm truly sorry Willie (Olga's younger brother) will not come to the wedding -- why not? It's no way between the two towns.

All right, will put the phone in the hall, think that's the best too. Dear, the name of our street in front of our home is Sten Sturegatan 25.

Yes Dear, I'm looking forward to the time we will not be very far away from each other, when we are spending the evenings together in our home. Dear, won't it be glorious?

Never Dear, my eyes will never be red from reading your sweet lines but perhaps you of

mine so will close this time with love to you, in heaps. I'm always your own loving, longing "baby" Folke
PS
Think Dear, Mrs. Dickson who lost her husband got a little girl the other day. She is quite happy now having a boy and a girl.

SEPTEMBER 15, 1909

Folke writes to Olga about those glorious, crisp September days we have in Sweden.

September 15, 1909
My Dearest Dearest,
Thanks Dearie for your postcard which I received this morning. I'm so happy when I receive a line from you even on a postcard.

Dearie, you can't imagine what fine weather we have now every day. The sun is shining from a bright blue ciel (sky). Hope Dearie we'll get just as nice weather on our honey moon. Dearie, I'm longing so after you and I'm really counting the hours till I can leave for Paris. We have been separated over a month and it seems like years!

Dearie, I have been to my men shop and ordered a lot of men things.

Workmen will begin to put linoleum flooring in the hall and kitchen corridor on Monday. Nothing more today and besides must go back to work.

Love to all and Dear, a long kiss to my sweet little darling so far away from me. I'm always with you and you've got my whole heart, your longing, loving "baby" Folke

SEPTEMBER 16, 1909

Folke finds it hard to kill time and he has invited some friends for bridge, his last time as a bachelor.

Folke had earlier said that it would "kill him" to postpone the marriage, Olga returns to the subject in a softer tone: *"I am marrying the truest little boy on earth, only I think we're marrying too soon"*. She was probably correct in that reflection, Olga and Folke were after all marrying only ten months after they met, but at the time, many favoured early marriages and they were probably carried away in that wave. Olga doesn't want to stop the marriage but perhaps just register the hesitation, or only air the subject a little. Folke reassures Olga not to be nervous, but does he know that Olga has no idea how babies are made? Probably not.

September 16, 1909
My own "Älskling" (Darling),
Must have a little talk with you but not very much news to tell you. First of all Dearie, thanks very much for your postcard from Waterloo. I'm sure Darling you're having a ripping time, I'm only so jealous <u>not to be with you</u>. It's not nice to say, but Dearie, I really don't know what to do, to "kill time".

Yes, today I've invited three of my friends to come home and have a game of bridge as I can't stay home alone every night, especially as my father went up to Stockholm last night to arrange something with Frej (Folke's brother) and in which school he is going to take now.

I'm quite sure that this bridge night will be the last for me as a bachelor and after that it will last very long before I invite people to come home and play bridge. Then <u>I have you</u>, and that <u>is better</u> than a million bridge nights.

When I saw papa off to Stockholm yesterday, we saw the sisters of Mrs. Kylenstierna. The next youngest is going to be married October 19th. Think Dear, if we will see them on our wedding trip.

Have been and ordered the carpet people to put in the linoleum on Monday. All our furniture are ready except the smoking room.

Yes Dearie, our day (18th) is coming nearer and nearer, but Dearie, don't be nervous, take it as calm as you can. I long for you so much Dearie but I would like to write more, but I have difficulties not knowing the proper English. What I write, comes right from the bottom of my heart.

I send my love to all. Dearie, believe me, I'm always your own true little loving, longing "baby"
Folke

SEPTEMBER 17, 1909

Folke surprises his friends by abstaining from alcohol and cigarettes.

September 17, 1909
Dearest my Darling,
Just a few lines to let you know I'm quite well but longing after you.

Dearie, the party yesterday came off very nicely and think Dearie, today I'm invited for another party to one of my friends. They think Dear, to see me before I get married.

Smoked one little cigar yesterday when all the others smoked big Havanas. Have not tasted a drop of alcohol. They laugh at me, but what do I care!! <u>I know who I want to please</u>. Dearie, I must have a shave and a brushing up so will sign off.

Love to all. I'm always your own loving, longing true ever your "baby"
Folke
xxxx xxxx

SEPTEMBER 18, 1909

Folke's letter to Olga in Brussels has been forwarded to 10 Rue Chalgrin, Paris.

Folke receives a card with Olga in a hat, probably not her best photo ever, but Folke is polite about it.

Folke reassures Olga, not to be nervous about the marriage. It would be so much better if he could be there to put his arms around her and do the reassuring that way.

Folke wants the flat to be as finished as possible and asks Olga many questions in great detail about lamps and chandeliers.

September 18, 1909
Dearest my own Darling Olga,
Since written yesterday you last night, I've received your postcard with your picture. Dearie, I had to look more than once to see who it was and found out it must be you "from the hat". Dearie, you are perfectly right, I liked it very much, I suppose it is just how you look now. Worried about wedding dresses etc.
 (There is a long discussion about chandeliers that I have left out)
Bought that blue china table set we looked at in the kitchen shop you remember. Papa is so nice he went with me. We also bought the sets for the wash stands. Hope you'll like them,.
Tell me what you think of it and your ideas if you don't like it. Dearie, tell me straight away what you think. Dearie, I'll do everything to get something you like.
Dearie, good night. Hope you'll not get very worried about this.
Love to all. Excuse my writing Dearie, but a bad pen.
XXX Kisses to you älskling (darling) from your own loving, longing "baby"
 Folke

SEPTEMBER 19, 1909
Folke has been so involved in furnishing the flat and, being the intense person that he is, he dreams of furniture and chandeliers all night.

Folke and his father went to the office after dinner on Sunday. It seems it was not unusual to go to the office even on a Sunday. He called the office Sunday morning to see if there was a letter for him then thinks there might be one in the afternoon. So mail must have come on Sundays too.

People in those days worked Saturdays and the idea of a "long weekend" did not exist. Doctors, we have been told, often took some time on their free Sunday to pop into the hospital and go "the round"to check on their patients. There did not seem to be the sharp division between work and being off work as we have today.

Folke writes that Sundays are heavy going and he is sad and longs so for his Olga and he ends his letter without the same flourish.

```
September 19, 1909
Dearest my own Darling Olga,
Since I wrote you last night, nothing to speak
of has happened or been done.
   When I left the office I passed the moving
picture and went in and had a look. Very good
program and I enjoyed it fairly well, not as
I did when you were with me in Paris and in
Brussels.
   When I came home, father and I spoke about
furniture, carpets, curtains and everything
and Dear, I dreamt about this the whole night.
Also chandeliers.
   I made a little embroidering but I have not
yet finished what I want to do. I slept this
morning until 10AM and when I had my breakfast,
father asked me to go out to Särö with him.
Dearie, I went and of course it began to rain.
We went home early and have just come in to the
```

office after we finished our dinner.

I telephoned this morning if there was any letter for me (Sunday?) but nothing and so I thought I might get one now but no, none.

Dearie, smoked a little cigar yesterday and a pipe today.

Father thanks you for your regards. Darling, you don't know how sad I'm today, simply for the reason that I'm longing so after you. Yes Darling, Sundays are so hard, but take a good long kiss from your own, ever,

Folke

1909
OLGA IN PARIS
CERTIFICATES AND PROMISES

To repeat, if two foreigners, wished to marry in Paris, one of them had to show proof of a 30 day residency in the city. That responsibility fell to Olga who travelled from Brussels to Paris. She left her family in Brussels where the parents were busy trying to find a suitable school for their son Willie. Olga travelled alone, unchaperoned and found it quite thrilling to arrive alone at the large railway station, Gare du Nord in Paris.

Olga stayed at 10, Rue Chalgrin, a "pension" in central Paris and this place was almost like "home" to her. She had lived there before with her family when she went to school in Paris. The owners of the pension welcomed her with open arms. They remembered her well and Olga wrote to Folke: *"they say I haven't changed at all and that I am the same lively terror"*.

This explains why she went there to live and not with one of the family friends, Mrs. Marshall or Mrs. Berthelot. Olga's mother later wrote that Olga should move to Mrs. Berthelot, but the independent Olga never complied, she stayed at this pension until Folke arrived in early October.

Olga wrote to Folke that she was given a very fine room: *"I have the sweetest little room on the first floor -- all in white and green -- some count had it, but they put me up anyway".*

Olga registered with the French police and visited the American consul to discuss the absence of a birth certificate. Officially Olga did "not exist" without a birth certificate and the lawyers had to "birth her" legally, and produce a substitute birth certificate, a process Olga thought quite silly.

SEPTEMBER 22, 1909

Maybe Folke had a little down period, because he had not written a letter the day before, unusual for him. But his spirits returned after receiving a letter from his Olga. She told him that she had gone to Paris for those important 30 days of residency before the wedding. Now they had to deal with invitation cards.

The subject of Olga's year of birth comes up yet again. It appears that she telegraphed 1891 and has since then, changed to 1890. This after all those repeated questions by Folke.

Olga has wisely decided that they should buy the chandeliers for their new flat together, when they are married and come home.

```
September 22, 1909
Dearest, Dearest Olga,
Thanks just lots making me so happy receiving
your letter telling me you were going to Paris
to settle the 30 days. Sweet little girl. Now
I'm anxious to hear from you Darling what you've
done. You can't understand how I've been longing
for four whole days for a letter from you. Yes
dear, I've been embroidering the whole time as
anything else couldn't interest me a bit, my
thoughts have been with you all day and night.
Haven't been able to sleep.
    Take care of yourself Darling, hope you've
```

arranged that you can count 30 days on to the 18th. Dearie, I'll come to Paris about the 10th with Papa. I'll not worry you at all, only help you if I can. I'm longing so after you.

Poor Willie, he never seems to come to a school he likes. Hope you'll succeed to get a good one for him.

Dearie, you telegraphed me 1891 and I just went to the church office and got advertised that we intended to marry. It has been done and I didn't know if I had to do it again with 1890 but after having asked them today, they told me that it's all right and I'll get the certificate with the correct date and year January 10, 1890. Never mind Dearie, I take with pleasure, a little trouble when it is for you.

About announcement cards, it's not necessary here to my friends. Only send <u>invitation</u> cards to enclosed people. They are my relations except Sternhagen and Lasse (Bratt). I expect only Lasse, my two brothers, father and perhaps one Sandberg to come and very well Dearie, they have to take the wedding as it will be.

It's only to let them know that we shall marry and show them that we have thought of them. You understand Dearie. I've written full names and titles to spare you trouble and none of them will come except the above names.

Dearie, I'm longing so after you. I can't tell you in words how much.

Very well Dearie, we'll wait to buy chandeliers till we come home or if we find any we like on our stay in Paris or on our honeymoon.

Dearie, hope you'll arrange about 30 days for the 18th of October. Or do we have to postpone it till the 20th or 21st? If you've been a clever girl, you've written an earlier date in the calender to avoid alterations.

Dearie, the flat is progressing and every day I'm adding something. It's such a lot to do but I wish you were here to help me Dearie. The embroidering is nearly finished. What a marvellous boy.

I've not smoked a single cigarette for nearly four weeks, a pipe and a little cigar sometimes, that's all.

Must work now so will close. Dearie, there's a kiss and believe me, it's from your loving, longing always your own "baby" Folke.

SEPTEMBER 23, 1909

The young Olga is all alone in Paris to arrange the wedding (her parents were stranded in Brussels searching frantically for a new school for her problematic brother, Willie).

Folke of course wishes that he could be by Olga's side to help with the arrangements.

September 23, 1909
Dearest, Dearest,
Heard from Ulrik you were alright in Paris. Dearie, how I wished I could have helped you and gone with you from Brussels to Smith etc. Dearie, I'm longing for you immensely and Dearie, my happiest time in my life will be when I marry you. I'll take care of you and you of me. Dearie, I'm thinking so much of you and everything I do is for you.

Darling, it is past 8PM and I'm quite alone in the office and the work is finished. Mr. Lundberg still on his honeymoon.

Darling, there is a kiss X--------

Smoked a little cigar yesterday, horrid, n'est-ce pas?

Of course Dear, you've to decide about invitations to Paris, friends like Cappelen, Marshall and others in the pension which you like. Understand?

Dearie, supper and father waiting so, ta-ta and kisses in thousands from your own always your longing, loving "baby" Folke

SEPTEMBER 24, 1909

Olga, who is arranging all the paper work for the wedding in Paris, has requested a complete list of all the various certificates for Folke to send. This is no easy undertaking. As she discovers the complexity of it all, she begins to wonder why they chose Paris to marry.

To further complicate matters, the Catholic bishop has earlier said that he will not let Olga marry in a Catholic church unless Folke agrees to bring the children up in the Catholic faith. So there is a lot for young Olga and Folke to consider.

There is to be a civil marriage and a Catholic church marriage and Folke wishes both to take place the same day. Olga was adamant that she wanted a simple wedding.

She, surprisingly, even contemplated wearing just travelling clothes and not a wedding dress at all. But Folke thinks she should have a wedding dress in church and Olga writes that her mother probably wouldn't allow her to marry in anything but a proper wedding dress. But Olga's thoughts are interesting because they say something about her character.

```
September 24, 1909
Dearest, Dearest Mimsie,
```
You've made me so happy today Dearie -- I received three long letters from you, Thanks so much for same.

I telegraphed you this afternoon that I'll get the certificates wanted, as soon as possible which is on Monday and then they have to be translated by the "Notarius Publicus" here and I suppose I can post them on to Tuesday or Wednesday.

I'll get my father and mother's marriage certificates, my mother's death certificate, my birth certificate, my baptismal certificate, and my confirmation certificate -- all of them.

But one certificate, most necessary, is the certificate stating that I'm libre (free) to marry, I cannot get before the 2nd of October. I'll bring that with me and Papa and I will leave for Paris in the first week of October.

If you want any more certificates, write me at once, don't spare on a wire (telegram), so I'll have time to obtain same.

All certificates will be translated into French. Hope to have your reply that I've understood the matter. My own little Darling, being alone in Paris, I wished myself there.

Dearie, from your letter I can understand that we can chose to marry at the Swedish legation or at the Mayor. Very well darling, can't this be done early in the morning and then have the Catholic marriage a few hours later? Could this be arranged, because marrying one day at the other place, and one at another place wouldn't be very nice. Or what do you mean Dearie?

For the marriage at the Mayor or Swedish legation, it would be nicest to have ordinary clothes, but dear, for the church wedding, don't you think you ought to have a wedding dress and I, a dress suit? Don't know the custom, but now you know my opinion. I'll bring both dress suit and tail coat.

Dearie, you'll understand that we'll come fairly early and can then arrange all this with you. But if you <u>also</u> think to have a wedding dress in church, you better order it, understand Dearie. You've a lot of trouble. I only wished I could be with you, but I will be in Paris in fourteen days.

If we have the marriage in the church in wedding dress, we can just as well be in the same clothes at the Mayor or the Swedish legation -- <u>just as you like Dearie. This is my answer frankly.</u> Hope you understand me quite.

All that you write to me about, is quite

livingly before me, just as when we were together in Paris. Everything makes me feel so good, all the past of my happiest time I've spent in Paris with you.

Madame Marshall, she is all the same good friend to us and give her my special regards. In fact, everyone in the pension. Where does your family intend to stay during the wedding? Please inform me if you are going to join them and if we could get rooms in the same pension or in the same hotel?

Dearie, I'm longing after you so much. Embroidering still and I have only a tiny bit left.

Have taken on a servant, looked very good and recommended by our old servant "Fina 699". I like her very much. Hope you'll do the same. Love to you from my father.

But Dearie, long kisses from your own always your loving "baby" Folke

SEPTEMBER 25, 1909
The flat is ready to receive the furniture and Folke will no longer be alone in the office as Lundberg is back from his honeymoon so Folke can spend more time at the flat.

September 25, 1909
My Dearest,
Just a few lines to let you know I'm going out shooting at Ingetorp in an hours time. Fine weather and I hope I have a good time.

Dearie, I'm longing immensely after you.

Just returned from our flat, all carpets on, furniture coming on Monday and Tuesday. I can then attend more to the flat, expecting Lundberg back at the office. I wish I were in Paris.

Went to Palace (restaurant) yesterday with Philip (Krafft) and we had a rather good time, waiting for the result of the election results for Parliament. Our candidate won with 50% more votes than the Socialist and Liberals.

My friend offered me brandy, whisky and the alcohol water but Dearie, I refused. No cigarettes yet and yesterday 2 cigars.

Must get home now, will write you further tomorrow night.

Dearie, there's some xxx---xxxx--- kisses you know from your "baby", loving and longing after you, ever Folke

SEPTEMBER 27, 1909

Olga, who is alone in Paris, tells Folke she was almost run over by a car. Folke is very worried when he imagines what could have happened. And to top it off, he thinks Olga flirts too much with "Quale" a friend of his in Paris.

Olga has told Folke that her mother wants her to move from the pension on 10 Rue Chalgrin, to a friend of theirs, Mrs. Berthelot. Olga's mother probably didn't think it proper that her unmarried and unchaperoned daughter lived by herself in a pension.

Folke is concerned that Olga might be angry with him for not having written a letter yesterday, the 26th, but he was hunting and was not able to mail it. He has after all written a letter every day since they parted early in August.

September 27, 1909
Dearest, Dearest Älskling (Darling),
Thanks Dearie, for your letter. I got it this afternoon Dearie and you really frightened me, how could you (almost) be run over? And Dearie, I think you flirt <u>too much</u> with Quale, but I know you <u>only</u> find him nice perhaps. Am I right älskling?

Dearie, do be careful for my sake only when you cross the streets. So you're moving from Rue

Chalgrin, I suppose to Mrs. Berthelot?

Dearie, I went out shooting Saturday afternoon and had just 2 hours in the lovely grounds and then the dark fell and I had to go to our shooting residence. I had good luck and shot 8 partridges for Toy (their dog). He was very good and not so very wild as usual.

Dearest, I'm so glad you've fixed the date to the 18th and no alterations. <u>Today, three weeks, I wont be so lonely as I'm!</u>, Dearie, I'm longing so after you.

Darling, I'm back to the flat this morning and Fina is there looking after everything until the new servant comes October 1st.

Dearie, you are probably very angry not having a letter from your baby yesterday but I came home too late from the shooting to get one posted.

I have been at the church office and got the certificate, then to the "translator publicus" and they will get it translated till Wednesday.

Is it all right, will you send an invitation to Arthur Hurtzig, Danford House, Alleyn Park, Dulwich, West London S.E. He is the friend of us who was over here with my brother. He will not come, but my brother is in love with his sister and then asked me if I couldn't get him invited and of course <u>we</u> can help him to that?

Late supper waiting. Kisses in lots from your always true little "baby" Folke

Smoked two small cigars yesterday. Regards to everybody.

SEPTEMBER 28, 1909

Olga has sent a telegram that she needs all the pertinent certificates urgently.

The furniture has been delivered to the flat and Folke couldn't be more pleased.

September 28, 1909
Dearest my Darling,
Dearie, since I wrote you yesterday I received your telegram wanting the papers immediately. Dearie, I confirm my telegram telling you that they will be posted tomorrow as the translator couldn't get them ready today.

You'll receive: my father and mother's marriage certificate, my mother's death certificate, my own birth, baptismal and confirmation certificate -- all these posted tomorrow.

On Monday I'll receive a certificate, let us call it, "marriage licence certificate" and I can't get that until Monday as it must be fifteen days after the little paper advertisement was dated. If you want that also at once, call it "licence" in a telegram you may send and I'll do everything to get it if possible.

Dearie, hope to hear that you understand how the matters stand and also anxious to hear if they reach you in time to get everything settled. Hope so Dearie.

All the furniture came to the flat this morning and they are simply grand.

Darling, lots to do so must ring off. Lots of kisses and believe me, I'm your own true little "baby" Folke

My kind regards to your family and all our mutual friends.

Your longing Folke

SEPTEMBER 29, 1909

The certificates are finally put in an envelope and sent to Olga in Paris.

A bachelor dinner is arranged for Folke by fifteen of his friends. Folke sent two letters and a telegram to Olga that day. Things were heating up!

September 29, 1909
REGISTERED MAIL Miss Olga Mims Dawson
c/o This Cook Sons,

1 Place de l'Opera
Paris France
Dearest, Darling,
Hope enclosed certificates will reach you safely. Will write more tonight. Must post them at once. Kisses and my whole heart,
   always your own
   Folke

September 29, 1909
Dearest, Dearest Mimsie,
Hear you have me again for the third time, first the papers, then the telegram and now this letter. You see Dearie why I tired you is because you'll have difficulties to get the registered letter at Cooks, but if you've asked Cook to help you get it, then I hope you'll get it all right.

   Papa wanted me to register the letter and I didn't want to do it, but when he got angry, telling me I didn't know that they could steal the letter, I gave in and now Dearie, it's not my fault if you have troubles with it.

   Dearie, I've spent most of the day in our flat. Everything seems to long for you Dearie. So do I.

   Tomorrow, fifteen of my friends are giving me a dinner (bachelor dinner) and Dearie, I'll think of you the whole time but cannot promise to not taste a brandy as probably everyone will be pressing me, and you know bachelor dinners.

   Regards to all. Hope to hear from you tomorrow.

   I'm always your own loving, longing "baby"
Folke

SEPTEMBER 30, 1909
This is the last day of September and Folke is off to his bachelor dinner.

September 30, 1909
Dearest my own girl,
In one hour I must be at the dinner my friends are giving or me.
Dearie, I'm longing so very much after you. I'm so eager to go to Paris, a week from now with father. My brother, the artist, is in Paris. If you see him, talk to him, don't know his address.

Dearie, write me a line soon. I'm longing to hear from you. I have no more time to spend as I'm not dressed.

Kisses in millions Dearie, and I won't forget you Dearie during the dinner. But surely they will try to make me happy or a little bit tipsy. I'm sure.

Dearie, I'm your own little loving, longing "baby" true as gold
Ever Folke
Love to all. When does your family arrive to Paris?

OCTOBER 1, 1909

We will not get the details of the bachelor party, because Folke will tell Olga all about it when he meets her in Paris, and we'll not be around to hear them.

October 1, 1909
Dearest Dearest Mimsie,
Thanks Dearie for your kind sweet letter which I received yesterday. Dearie, hope you received the papers in time.

Had a very nice time yesterday at my bachelor dinner, you will hear when I come to Paris how we spent it.

Dearie, which are the promises I have to give to the priest?

Well, I won't trouble you more about the wedding until we are in Paris a week from tomorrow. I'm longing to take you in my arms.

Papa wishes about 50 cards for the church

to send them to his best friends over here and
about 5-6 persons in Paris. You understand.
 Everything of this will be settled to our
satisfaction when we are in Paris. Dearie, good
bye, must work. Love to all. But to you Darling,
I send my best love and kisses in lots. I'm
always your own true little baby Folke

OCTOBER 2, 1909

Folke's departure for Paris is getting nearer and the flat is fitted with electricity. Nice to know that they enjoyed the comfort of electricity, but they probably did not have the comfort of a WC. When thy got their next and larger flat in 1913, they were very excited then to have "a glorious WC" . So I doubt there was a WC in this flat. The sewers in Gothenburg had only been connected for water toilets since 1907 and Folke and Olga's flat was then on the "outskirts" of central Gothenburg. Today the flat would be considered extremely central.

Folke thinks that after they meet in Paris and marry, there will never be any more separations like this one. But that is wishful thinking. Lucky for him he didn't not know what was to come in 1913.

October 2, 1909
Dearest Dearest Darling,
Thanks just heaps for your postcard which I
received this afternoon. Dearie, my heart and
soul are with you and I'll be in Paris Saturday
or Sunday, we leave Gothenburg on Thursday next.
 Dear, I spent the whole day long in our flat
trying to put everything in order, but Dearie,
when we are there together, we can arrange it
over and over again till we like it.
 Wonder how and when I'll meet you. Will
telegraph when we will arrive. Dearie, you are
very much missed in the nice little flat. Dearie,

when I rest in the comfortable chairs I am listening for you Dear.

All right, in a week we will be together and then never any hard separation like this. Will write or telegraph if you shall take rooms for us. Thanks.

Goodbye for now dear, I must go back to our flat to see to the electric men. Kisses in millions and my kindest love to all.

I'm your own true little baby always the same loving, longing Folke

OCTOBER 3, 1909
Folke always used a gentle tone with Olga.

October 3, 1909
Dearest my own Olga,
Today it's Sunday, the last <u>long Day</u> I'll be alone Dear. I've finished working in the office, but I have come here to the office to see if any letters from you.

Dearie, this morning a parcel arrived (from a Mr. Edwards at Herbert Villa, Charlton Kings, Cheltenham who appeared to have been invited to the wedding) with this letter which I hand over now. The parcel was torn to pieces, that's why I opened it and Dearie, you received a lovely hand painted cloth with pink roses and it will be simply charming in our salon. Dearie, I'm sure you don't mind that I opened same as it was impossible to forward, but I'm sure you like to see it, so I'll take the present with me if you want to show it to your friends in Paris.

Papa and I will go to our saw mill and this afternoon. I'll go and look to our flat and pack things at home (his father's place) which I like to have at home (the new flat).

Dearie, the days are not many before I'll be in Paris. You don't know how much I'm longing for you. Can't sleep, only thinking, thinking of you Dear, day and night.

Papa wants to leave now, so good buy for today with millions of kisses from your own, true little baby Folke

OCTOBER 4, 1909

The promise to bring up their children in the Catholic faith, a prerequisite for the marriage according to the Catholic bishop, is something Folke agrees to because he loves Olga, and he has sent a telegram to that effect. His reasoning seems mature and sensible.

In retrospect, however, neither Olga nor Folke were particularly "religious". Olga, in her old age, hardly ever went to church, nor did Folke. However, they were very moral, honest individuals, caring and generous to others -- whatever their station in life. What better way to be a "Christian"?

October 4, 1909
Dearest my own Mimsie,
Thanks Dearie for your letter received this morning, You see Dearie, I've telegraphed you yes, that I consent to give the promise that if we are blessed with children, they are going to be brought up Catholic. Dearie, we will talk it over when I can speak a little better with you, but you see, I agree because I love you so very much. I know Dearie you are not one asking me to give a promise like this one, that's the church and Dearie, I'm putting your religion just as high as mine. Dearie, no more about this until we are together.

Darling, I've spent the day by running from the church office, the translator and the flat. The flat is darling, I hope you'll find the same. Now nearly in order, but Dearie, there's a lot of things to do when we come back.

Dearie, you'll have about 50 invitation cards for the church ready when we come to send them off at once. If there are more than 50, it doesn't matter as we have lots to send to. Hope you've sent invitations to the names given earlier.

Good night and pleasant dreams from your own little baby, longing as Ever Folke

OCTOBER 5, 1909

Folke wants Olga to book rooms at her pension at 10, Rue Chalgrin in Paris for him and his father.

Folke travels with his father, and the two of them are very close. It's just those two on this journey and Folke must have wished that his beautiful mother Ragnhild, who died very young, could be with him on this journey. Wouldn't she have loved his Olga?

October 5, 1909
Dearest my own Olga,
Dearie, here you have me again, just as usual, the same Folke.

Dearie, today a tiny little package arrived from England. It says, "Please forward", but as I'm leaving the day after tomorrow, I'll bring it with me. I have received two nice presents, I can't explain as I don't know the names, but you'll see them when we come home.

Dearie, I can't in words explain how I'm longing for you, even if you are very busy. Hope not so very much that you can't spare me a few minutes for me.

If you ask Madame Petiot (at the pension at 10 Rue Chalgrin where Olga was still staying) to reserve two rooms for Papa and me. Would you trouble about this, for Saturday evening or Sunday. One each. That is, if you are still there. Understand Dearie?

We will probably lay over in Cologne. You'll be receiving a telegram when we will be in Paris.

I must close, having a lot to do. Good buy and regards to all. Kisses xxx--- in lots from

your longing, loving, baby Folke
 Smoking hardly anything. A quarter of a pipe today and 1 cigar yesterday.

OCTOBER 6, 1909

The last letter before leaving for Paris. I am happy for my grandfather, that he was finally able to marry my grandmother. They had waited long enough and poor Folke had probably suffered the most during this absence.

October 6, 1909
Dearest Dearest,
Here you have me again, a tiny note the last letter for this time. Dearie, as Papa and I are leaving tomorrow for Dear Paris, where you are. Dearie, we will arrive on Saturday about 4PM. Hope to meet you that day and not like in Brussels, resting a whole night knowing that you were not more than a few yards from me.
 Dearie, I have thousands and thousands of things to do so excuse the bad writing.
 Please have the cards for church ready for us to send off to friends as it is in the last moment to send them off. Hope you have sent to the names given. Did I give you aunt Axeline Carlsson's address : Sveagatan 25, Göteborg.
 Dearie, must close with my best love to all.

 Dearie, take the very best kisses, you know I'm your own little "baby" Folke, always loving and longing for the girl he loves so much.

1909
FINALLY MARRIED

Since Olga and Folke would be together from now on, there are no letters from Folke to Olga to tell us what happened in Paris when Folke finally was able to hold Olga in his arms again. We can only imagine the wedding and the honeymoon.

We can also only guess about the rest, the return of the happy couple to their fine flat on Sten Sturegatan 25 in Gothenburg.

I would have liked to know a lot of things -- what Olga thought of the flat that Folke had arranged and how she liked the household staff that he had selected, and what they thought of Olga. How long did it take Olga to learn Swedish? How did Olga adapt to the Swedish winter and the flat, which was heated with firewood in tiled ovens. It was, after all, only 1909, one hundred and fifteen years ago.

I'm sure Folke and his father Axel were happy to have a woman in their lives again. And Olga was a charmer and what I have gathered from reading Olga and Folke's letters, Folke's father, Axel, quite doted on his charming and pretty daughter in law.

Olga's mother had a great fondness for Folke, too, and came to spend much time with them in Sweden when she was widowed (1916). After all, it was this side of the Atlantic where the grandchildren were produced. Olga had a steady stream of them. By the time she was 32 she had eight children, with one more to go.

When Olga and Folke returned to Gothenburg from the wedding in Paris in 1909, they settled happily in their beautiful new home and it did not take long for Olga to be pregnant and a year after that, pregnant again. Two children followed in close succession.

Olga must have welcomed some rest after the two children, surely a little intermission between childbirths would be expected.

That might be what Olga had wanted, but the lady was very fertile and Folke so very much in love and so eager and...

1912
OH, NOT PREGNANT AGAIN !

SEPTEMBER 4, 1912
By 1912, Olga at twenty-two had already had two children, Anita, two, and Billy, one year -- only twelve months apart.

Olga's parents had spent the summer with Olga and Folke by the sea at Särö and they planned to take their daughter with them on a little vacation when they left in August. They no doubt felt that Olga deserved some time alone away from the children so they took her on a tour to Germany on their way back to Belgium (they would later return to Jacksonville in Florida).

Berlin, as now, was a large and luxurious city, so much more lavish and full of wonderful things than little Gothenburg and Olga's father was looking forward to spoiling his daughter. In Berlin he bought Olga a set of Alaska fox furs (for 400 marks) plus many other fine things.

I am glad they had this wonderful time together in glittering Berlin. Who could possibly imagine that two years later, Germany would be immersed in a war, World War I, and that Olga's father William Dawson, would die four years later from cancer.

Olga, at this time had two small children, she did not feel strong enough for another pregnancy. She was worried that she was behind with her period and being always very regular, she wrote to Folke that she was very concerned. If she was pregnant again, it would certainly spoil this vacation in Germany she told Folke.

In Berlin the family visited a cousin of Olga's (on her mother's side) who was married to a doctor Lerch, an inventor of a very promising improved X-ray system, as Olga wrote to Folke. As a doctor he had told Olga that she should not have another child so soon. It could be too risky.

Olga wrote to Folke and told him what her cousin had said and that this cousin and her husband had both taken a fancy to her and had asked her to take down her hair, a rather intimate thing in those days and that they were both "enraptured" as Olga expressed it, with her long lovely hair. They had never seen anything like it.

When Olga found that she indeed was pregnant again she became alarmed and wrote a desperate letter to Folke while feeling very ill. It is for Olga an unusually frank letter and something that I think, should not be censored. After all, Olga saved the letter for all those years, and she also saved what Folke wrote back. If she had wanted those letters destroyed, she would have done it a hundred years ago and they would not be lying to the left of me today in 2014, being copied into a computer.

Olga admitted to being *"miserable and sick as a dog"*. She thought another pregnancy would hurt her:

"You talk about if it's Gods wish, it will not hurt me. Well, why was your mother taken away so early -- only because her children sapped all her strength. I hate to write all this, but it's what I feel. I've been ill all day, cold as ice and can't eat anything and I feel like ending my existence.

Well I'm a cat to write you all this and make you

miserable, but it's just how I feel.

Don't worry, I will be home about the ninth or tenth of September. Shall make it as short as possible."

Olga appears to become more composed later in the letter and speaks how much she misses her children at home and ends the letter *"Good bye my sweetheart, forgive me if I've been mean. Your loving wife, Olga"* A few days later she seems more comfortable with the idea of another pregnancy. She writes the next day how she remembers the happiness they both felt when their first child Anita was born.

Gothenburg September 4th, 1912
Mrs, Olga Jonsson
c/o Thos Cook Son
Stefanplatz 2
WIEN
Dearest own Precious Darling Olga,
Thanks for your last letter from which I find, that you feel miserable and you made me too miserable and sorry for writing all that. Can I help it? No. No dear, the "skjöljning" (rinse) must not have done it's duty, an accident must have happened.

Dear, don't think that I wanted a child when you do not feel strong enough and don't want one. My love to you is stronger than that and the last thing in the world I wished, is to see you suffer or feel bad.

On Tuesday I wired Savoy asking for your address where to forward my letters also some to your parents from Una and Willie but got no reply, but suppose you had left.

Yesterday I got your wire from Marienbad and sent one in answer that all well at home and asked again where to send letters. I do not know where to send this one as I have no answer, but shall wait and mail it before I hear from you, but I hope darling that you are not too sick to write.

Anita's (their eldest daughter) birthday was

celebrated as quiet as it could be done without "Mama" at home. I brought out a little house with lots of animals, a "Noa's House" if you know what that is. Also a boat, a spade and a bucket. Papa bought her a ball. Willie got her "en skramla"(rattle) which she liked very much.

Papa went out with me and we had dinner together in our home. In the afternoon I went for supper to Folke and Helfrid and stayed with them, alone until 12PM.

Axel (Folke's brother) is much better and improving fine. Karin Pripp is also doing fine. So far no new cases at Särö. Just phoned and the babies are fine.

I have some work to do so will continue before sending this one off.

Cheer up darling and be sure that I will welcome you home with open arms as I'm longing very very much.

Thanks darling for your letter which came now, telling me that you were leaving Berlin. Darling, let me know if you get this letter. I will mail it to Cook Vienna as I believe you will be there. I will forward all mail there instead to Marienbad as I think you will not stay long in Marienbad.

Wire me when you leave and which way etc. Hope you you will come back soon. Love from all at Särö.

Kisses to you from the babies and myself and kindest regards to your parents.

Your own true loving
Folke

If your money is quite finished, let me know where to send some as I do not want you to be without.

SEPTEMBER 4TH, 1912
In the same envelope -- A small folded note. No date.
Personal!
Rif sönder det efter läsning (tear up after reading).

The note has no date, most likely written in the evening after Folke wrote his letter in the office earlier in the day and been put in the same letter as he had kept it, waiting for the address. At home, maybe after a brandy, he allowed himself to speak more intimately. Folke interprets what Olga has written as though she intends to have an abortion in Germany with the help of her relative, the German doctor, and he tries to calm and reassure her. She never did tear up the note as instructed. So here it is.

My poor little own precious Darling,
I can very well understand that you are anxious about you know, but sweetheart, first of all be sensible and don't go and ruin yourself for lifetime. Better that you come home soonest possible and we will go to Dr. Mannheimer and let him examine you, then see what he says and if there is the least danger for yourself Darling to go through another eight months (one already past) it is his duty to take it away if it is your positive wish, because neither you nor I would like to be "murderers". But dear, it is not "murder" to prevent children when, or if it is any risk of the mother's life.
   Don't worry dear, enjoy the few days you have left in Germany and we will see what to do when you come back to your longing and loving true husband.
   One thing Dear, our good God who has given us each other and also our precious small babies, would not I am sure, give you a baby if it would hurt you, we live only for each other and the

children like a loving wife and husband and a happy family.

Dear, I quite agree with you that it must be dreadful to go through another P.D.W (?), but darling, come home quick and we will see what to do. But don't go to any German doctors, they will kill you and I should get crazy if you did, because they only do it for taking the money and I want to be near you if you do anything like that.

Don't worry your father and mother.

An hour long kiss, your own little baby Folke

***

The pregnancy resulted in a beautiful child, Mary Carita, borne in May 1913. As fate had it, the little baby Mary Carita came to play an important role in Folke's life that same year -- the newly born child was Folke's only family when Olga and the children Anita and Billy left on a very long trip in 1913.

1913
PLEASE COME HOME DARLING OLGA!

In September 1913, Olga and their two children, Anita, three and Billy, two, and the nanny, nurse Ida, set out on a journey to Jacksonville, Florida, where they would visit Olga's parents. The four months old Mary Carita would stay behind with Folke, looked after by a nurse.

Folke waved them off at the railway station in Gothenburg Sweden. Their destination was Hamburg where they all would embark on a Hamburg America Line ocean liner, the newly built, super luxurious IMPERATOR, the largest ocean liner in the world. The destination was New York. From there a train would take them to Jacksonville.

But first they would spend the night in a Hamburg hotel where Olga wrote her first letter to her dear Folke. She would also send him telegrams at various points during their travel, to let him know of their safe arrivals at these points. Her letters to Folke were many and loving, but not as many as he wrote to her, not always dated and not so interestingly written as his letters were -- and not as long. In New York, she and the children spent the night at The Broztell Hotel before commencing the train ride to Jacksonville in Florida.

Folke was extremely concerned to see his darling wife and two children leave that day at the railway station in Gothenburg. Any sane man would be terrified under such circumstances -- his precious wife and two children were to go on the same ocean where, just the year before, in 1912, the Titanic had sunk on its maiden voyage from England to New York. As many as 1,514 people had drowned in the icy water after the enormous, luxurious liner collided with an iceberg. One year later, his wife and children were travelling on the same route, on the same ocean full of treacherous icebergs.

Folke had reluctantly agreed to Olga leaving, as her declared "intention", which he took as a "promise", was that she and the children would return before Christmas. That would mean being without them for two and a half months, but he thought he could cope, knowing that they would be back for Christmas. This was his consolation.

On board the vessel, Olga wrote that the Hamburg America Line officials had asked her many questions. Why, at only twenty-three, had she two children? Olga never knew whether she was born 1890 or 1891, and she had apparently first said that she was 22 and they could not believe that she had two children at that young age. Did she have any proof that these children were hers? She did not -- passports were not necessary at that time. They became mandatory after the First World War.

They might also have wondered where her husband was -- this was, after all, 1913. Women did not yet have the right to vote and it was not common for independent women travelling the high seas alone. She was probably wise not to mention that besides these two young children aged three and two, she had a four months old baby left behind in Gothenburg, with her husband and a nurse. It might have given an unfavorable impression. Who can blame the Germans for asking a few questions.

After all, my twenty-three year old grandmother did not fit the usual pattern of a wife at that time. And she was an American!

However, the journey was successful, the service was excellent on board and Olga's two children were much praised for looking so wonderfully and remarkably healthy. There were endless comments, how cute they were, what lovely colouring they had, and what Olga fed the children. The children who had spent the summer outdoors and by the ocean at the family summer house, "Villa Florida" at Särö, were probably nicely tanned and healthy looking.

Nurse Ida was young and very pretty and much admired and had to escape below deck to get away from her ardent admirers, a Swedish steward and a Danish waiter, as reported by Olga.

For people travelling to America today, in cramped airplanes, it is hard to imagine how luxuriously spacious liners crossing the oceans at that time actually were. For years, shipping companies in Germany and England had competed to build the fastest and most desirable vessels. By 1913, the race had reached its peak and there were a number of enormous pleasure palaces crossing the Atlantic.

There were many large vessels and we tend to remember the Titanic because it collided with an ice berg and sank, but it had two sister ships called the Olympic and the Gigantic (renamed the Brittanic, in order not to remind people of the Titanic). But these three British ships were already too small and far behind when the first, the Titanic, was launched in 1912.

The Germans in fierce competition with the British, had learned a lot from the Titanic disaster and launched the spectacular SS Imperator in 1913 and later two similar sister ships, the SS Vaterland

(Father Land) and the SS Bismarck. They were the best, biggest and most luxurious in the world. On board the Imperator, a large oil painting of the German emperor in full figure, military dress, proudly dominated the majestic staircase. This was an era when countries seemed stable, but devoted their energies to nationalism, competition for colonies and military expansion. The frothy shipbuilding race was part of this dangerous game that only a year later led to the First World War.

Who at that time could have foreseen, that there would be a world war that Germany would lose and that six years later, the Imperator, this newly launched, glorious marvel of a vessel with the German emperor, proudly posing from his portrait over it's majestic staircase, would be transporting American troops back from the war in Europe in 1920. And who at that time could have foreseen that the glorious Imperator would one day be given to the English Cunard line, as war reparations after the First World War, most likely as payback for the German torpedoing of the British Lusitania in 1915.

Such thoughts could not have entered any sane person's mind in 1913. Besides, everything seemed just fine as Olga and her children, Anita and Billy and nurse Ida were in Hamburg, ready and very eager to board the largest ship in the world, the massive Imperator, the pride of Germany destined for New York. Everything seemed just fine then, just fine.

In first class, the interiors were as opulent as a palace in London or Hamburg. Olga and her fellow passengers on the Imperator left their lavishly appointed cabins and climbed the magnificent gilded staircases to the many palatial rooms -- such as a "Ladies Salon and Library", a Tudor style hunting-lodge-like "Men's Smoking Room", a two story domed dining room seating 700 people, and the "Daytime Social hall" which was converted into a Ball room at night. There was also a "Winter Garden" and a gymnasium. For the wealthiest passengers there were suites with verandas and personal servants and they could also rent private dining rooms, or dine at the exclusive Ritz Carlton restaurants.

I suppose our unafraid Olga would have been anxious to pay a visit to the much talked about feature of the Imperator, the absolutely magnificent "Pompeian Swimming Pool" and sure enough, she wrote to Folke at the end of the journey about a "perfectly adorable swimming pool" and that she had been in the pool twice and had learned how to swim on her back. She did have a nanny to mind the children and being a woman on her own, would probably have chosen to visit between 10:30 and 12:30, during the "Ladies only" hours.

Olga no doubt enjoyed the salty water in the Pompeian Swimming Pool. She was used to swimming in the ocean at their summer house on the coast and a special water pipe had been installed from the sea to the bath tub in their upstairs bathroom in villa Florida at Särö, to bring salt water indoors.

The ship's Pompeian swimming pool was the first ever swimming pool on a vessel, and the pool, 10 by 30 meters with columns, mosaic, luxurious bathing huts must have been sensational, especially when you consider that in 1913, the city of Gothenburg, Olga and Folke's home, had only six years earlier, in 1907, been the first city in Sweden to connect water closets (toilets) to the sewer system.

The ocean voyage would take around six days, possibly a bit faster depending on the weather.

Twenty-three knots were enough and why rush the trip when you travelled in such splendour?

Some shipping companies, in the race to build the "best" ship, had prioritized speed but the engines had often been too noisy for the passengers so Hapag Lloyd who owned the Imperator, had made the strategic decision to emphasize comfort before speed, and by 1913, their vessels had the best of both.

Folke might have been pleased to know, and he might possibly have found it out before he let his family travel, that the Imperator had improved warning systems against approaching ice bergs and had been outfitted with double hulls that would save the vessel from sinking, should it, against all odds, collide with an iceberg.

Ice bergs had been much on the minds of people around the globe after the Titanic collision only a year earlier in 1912. Ice bergs were like floating mines that could sink ships and kill thousands. So the German ship builder could not risk the lives of the five thousand people (passengers and crew combined) on board the Imperator.

Some might wonder how Olga could leave her four months old daughter, Mary Carita, behind and bring her two other small children to Florida. Some might also wonder why Olga was reluctant to come home before Christmas as promised. Wouldn't two months absence be enough? Did she not miss her Folke and her little baby Mary Carita? Folke kept asking this question over and over as he passionately sent a letter at least every other day, to his dear Olga c/o her parents house in Jacksonville, Florida.

Olga's parents had invited Olga and the children and had also paid for their trip. This visit was very important to Olga. She was after all only twenty-three years old, had been married to her husband Folke for four years and had during those four years, three children.

Olga no doubt needed a rest after that early marriage and the three children one after the other. There must also have been a strain in adapting herself to her Sweden. She deserved some time alone for awhile and a pause in all those pregnancies. In 1913, she got an extra four months of "freedom" when she was physically away from fertile Folke. But after that, she had a baby every eighteen months until she was 32 years. At 32, she had born eight children -- an age when many people these days have their first child.

She declared when she left in September, that she had the intention of returning with the two children before Christmas and that would have meant a vacation for two months. In her correspondence with Folke she explains that she thinks this might be the last time she will have a chance to go home to her native Jacksonville, and one wonders why she had such a feeling. She was young and her father was still a youngish man and in good health.

Olga's father, William Dawson, had recently bought Greenfield Plantation, a 1000 acre plantation in Jacksonville and he must have been very enthusiastic in his letters and no doubt wanted his dear (perhaps favourite) daughter to see the new house he was building there. The original house on the plantation had been burned to the ground during the Civil War by the Union army. Her father also intended to buy a great number of farm animals. Perhaps this appealed to Olga. After all, there were more things to life than having babies.

Olga begs her husband Folke to be patient and let her stay over Christmas. She wants to see her father's house completed before she leaves. Or could there possibly have been some other reason she wanted to stay so long?

Olga writes that this separation is "by fate" and their hearts will only have grown fonder when she returns. She writes, without mentioning any details, that she felt that she and Folke had become "estranged during the summer". None of that is mentioned in Folke's letters except that he writes that the four years with her have been the best and happiest in his life and that he cannot believe that they have quarrelled at times, but never again!

I am glad that my young grandmother braved it and went to see her father and mother in September 1913. There actually was something to that feeling of hers that she should visit them.

Only six months after she came back to Sweden, the First World War broke out and continued until 1918. Sadly, her father fell ill and died in 1916, and Olga was prevented from returning to visit him during his illness, or to travel to his funeral in 1916. It was too risky.

German submarines might torpedo passenger ships as they had done with the Lusitania, a year earlier in 1915. So it was, indeed, fate working in many different ways. Imagine how Olga would have grieved, had she not gone back to see her father in 1913. And Folke might have felt worse if he had not let her go. That was not the last time Olga visited Florida, but it would be the last time she would see her father alive.

In 1913, or any time for that matter, it would seem unusual for a wife to leave her husband with her two such small children, and Olga was aware of this and asked Folke in a letter in October what people said about her being gone so long.

Her mother Anita, had already written to Folke,

thanking him for his sacrifice in letting his wife come and visit the family in Florida. She tried to point out to Folke that she and her husband would have their daughter Olga for a very short time, whereas he would have Olga all his life. That was not much consolation judging from Folke's letters. He suffers terribly and he would never had let Olga and the children go if he had known how painful the loneliness would be.

Some might think that Folke's missing Olga is strange, but Edwardian society that he and Olga lived in had its roots directly into Victorian thinking and motherhood was the pure, life-giving and harmony-producing centre of the house. If the mother, the vital centre suddenly left the home and embarked on a journey across the globe, there had, inevitably, to be an enormous emptiness left behind. And this was Folke's experience. He did not know how to fill the void except with constant longing for his wife and the other children. His days were fairly routine, his time in the office and his time in the morning and his evenings with Mary Carita, their four months old baby. His days proceeded like molasses and the weeks without Olga seemed like months.

Olga wished that Folke would go out more, and see friends and relatives in order to pass the time. The extremely handsome Folke would have been welcome anywhere. Alas, seeing other people did not do it for him -- he wanted his wife and children back. There was no other consolation.

Folke was not a great reader, and yes, he went to the moving pictures, enjoyed golf and cards, but this was no substitute for his darling wife.

In Jacksonville, Olga's parents were intent on making a wonderful homecoming for Olga. They arranged trips to the beach in their motor car, Olga met old friends and the evenings were mostly spent out. No wonder her sense of time was actually the direct opposite of Folke's, as is seen here in one of her letters: *"the days seem to whirl by, think I've been away from home two months, it hardly seems so long. I suppose I've so much to do that I haven't time to think, but darling, I will be glad to get home to my own little cosy happy home and you sweet darling. Now be a man and let me remain here over Xmas, it's nearly here and January will come before you know it"*

That is easy for Olga to say, but poor Folke explains to her that he chooses to walk the back streets in Gothenburg to avoid being seen and pitied by friends and relatives for being abandoned by his wife for all those months. It only makes it worse and he invariably begins to cry when they try to commiserate with him. So he avoids these meetings in the streets as best he can. That he truly suffers is evident in his nervous stomach condition.

It worries Folke that if Olga stays over Christmas, her parents will convince her to stay for her birthday in January and then for Easter and then God knows what. If she gets used to staying away, she might leave him altogether. Folke's imagination runs riot. He has no way of coping with his worries and develops a nervous stomach condition and the family doctor is concerned and writes to his father. If Folke is going to spend the entire Christmas and New Year period alone, it will make his condition much worse.

Something must be done. And right away.

***

SEPTEMBER 29, 1913

Olga and her children began their journey from Gothenburg on September 23, 1913 and Folke wrote his first letter September 26, 1913. It was the only one in Swedish, all the others are in English, and since this book is in English, I have chosen to start with the first English letter three days later.

When Folke begins this letter, he is happy to have received three loving letters from Olga on board the German ship SS Imperator. She tells him of seeing large boats and many sailing ships on the way to Southampton (from Hamburg) where the ship picked up more passengers while an orchestra entertained passengers on deck. Olga's main interest was in the people she met on board and their many comments about her healthy children: "Now isn't that just a little Dutch picture" and "Oh, isn't she a pretty thing, what lovely curls". People told her that such lovely children are seldom seen in America.

Olga writes that she is "sick of being on the water", most likely because the SS Imperator was top heavy and made the ship sway considerably. Attempts were made to rectify this problem when it was docked and repaired the following month.

Olga naturally longs for Folke and it is obvious she realized that there were many risks involved with this journey as she wrote these lines: *"Do you miss me much Dear? Oh I do hope you love me and that this separation will not prove fatal to our home life."*

Folke wrote this and many other letters on his company's stationary, Jonsson, Sternhagen & Co., a large export company owned by his father, Axel Jonsson, a very successful Gothenburg businessman. This is where Folke spent his days when Olga was gone. The company had, among other things, made a lot of money selling timber in the form of laths used for building houses and pit props used for mines -- exported to an expansive and powerful England with all its colonies, at that time intact. The letter was typed and contains Olga's name and address, probably how he used to write business letters. His other letters to Olga at this time were in his own meticulous handwriting and a joy to peruse. Olga was staying with her parents on 115 East Adams Street in Jacksonville, and if anyone is tempted to Google the address, I can reveal that the old family house is no longer there but has been replaced by a very public looking building.

```
September 29, 1913
Mrs. Olga Jonsson
c/o W.B Dawson, Esq.
115 East Adams Street
Jacksonville Florida U.S.A
```

My own Dearest Darling,
I am so glad today to receive three nice sweet letters from you my dear, and feel much better to know that you are so comfortable on board s/s Imperator. Well darling, you can understand that I am lonely. Although I am very much engaged by everyone, I don't like that business. I would very much prefer to come home and stay with you dear. Saturday we had a very good fishing day. Left Gothenburg at 12.00 and came home by 7 at night. We caught a lot of mackerels and whiting. I myself got fourteen mackerels and twenty-five whiting. Afterwards we had supper at Mr. Halling and played card until 1 at night.
 Yesterday I was out playing golf the whole day, but was not successful. Hope to be better today on the course, where I am going to leave in about an hour. You see, there is not much left for me to attend to except the moving of the furniture from our old flat. I was over there 2 hours this morning and luckily we have fine sunshine and a suitable day for moving. Tonight I am invited to Grand Hotel to Ivar Lignell, he

is giving a dinner there for Mr. Hegel and some others. I don't know yet who are coming along.

Well dear, now you have heard what I have been doing. Mary Carita is so fine, her stomach fine and yellow, she has got a very fine appetite and eats up her whole bottle. I see her every morning, dinner and night and she is quite sad when I leave her. She is out every day 3-4 hours. The nurse is very nice and takes care of our Mary Carita. The nurse takes her private walk almost every day after Mary Carita is taken care of and has had her bottle and she returns for supper at 8PM. Britta looks after Mary Carita while the nurse is out, but so far, Mary Carita has not been awake after her supper meal while the nurse is out.

Thanks for your telegram from Cherbourg, I was so glad to get it.
Well now I must go to lunch before I go to Hovås. Kisses in millions to you all dear, and hug the small angels from me and take good care of you all. Glad to hear nurse Ida (the Swedish nanny) had some company on board.
Well, a long sweet kiss from your own loving true husband Folke.
Excuse my bad English -- Don't show this letter to anybody.

OCTOBER 2, 1913
It does not take many days on his own for Folke to start missing Olga. When she returns they will move into a new larger flat at Berzeliigatan 26 in Gothenburg, only a block away from the old flat. Folke is overseeing its renovation.

Olga was breast-feeding when she left and Folke wants to know if the milk has stopped and delicately asks if she has had her period.

October 2, 1913
My Dearest own Darling,
Another day passed and office work finished. It's six o'clock and I have time to write you a few lines.

Mary Carita, our little angel is surely longing and missing Mama so far away from us, and I'm on her side, it is dreadful to be alone here without you dears. Yesterday alone at Avenyn with Papa and Ruth (his sister) and we three played cards until 10 when we went to bed. Dearest, tears came dripping from my eyes when I said my prayers for you all so far away, apart -- last night.

Don't mention anything about my feelings as your parents cannot understand that, as of course they will tell you all sorts of things to persuade you to stop as long as possibly.

I'm lonesome, just feeling a half person, not even that I'm feeling like crying out as a baby. And so you have not sent me a wireless as you promised -- I'm waiting for one every minute. Hope nothing happened you all. That would kill me on the spot. How is your breast and have you got "you know"?

Write me soon every day dear and take care when crossing streets. I'm thinking of you every minute. No news to write about, nothing happened. Uncle Oscar was up for dinner and sent his regards.

Olga sweetheart, come home soon to your own true husband. Kiss the two darlings, send my greetings to nurse Ida, and also your parents, Una (Olga's sister) & Willie (Olga's brother) and Bob (Una's fiancee).

Kisses from us both here at home.
Your ever true loving
    Folke

OCTOBER 6, 1913
Folke is anxiously waiting for a telegram from Olga in New York. Telegrams were extremely important at that time. Folke feels so terribly far away from her and with the limited ways of communicating, one can understand his frustration. Phones were used for local calls and far from everyone had them. Telegrams were the only quick way of communicating over a long distance in those days and the year before, in 1912, Olga and Folke had witnessed the massive and impressive government "Telegraph Building" built at great expense in their hometown of Gothenburg. Lucky for them, cables for sending telegrams between Europe and America had been laid on the ocean floor by this time but, as an operator had to send the messages by hand, it was costly -- there was limited space on those cables and abbreviations were necessary. Sometimes Olga and Folke used "codes" which meant certain things, but that comes later in their correspondence.

Olga had in a previous letter asked that the nurse would take out Mary Carita, her little baby, every day for several hours, even in the winter. Folke is happy to report that is taken care of.

```
October 6, 1913
My own dearest darling Olga,
Thanks for your telegram which I received
yesterday when I came home from golf. You do
not know my dear how glad I was to know that you
all arrived safely in New York. Sweetheart I'm
now longing for some long nice letters from you,
telling me all about your trip. Mary Carita is
fine and she has been out to Slottskogen (large
park in Gothenburg) today. She was quite rosy
when she came home, smiled and laughed when I
took my talking time with her which is at least
an hour a day. Darling, she is so sweet but
```

missing you. We all are -- you bet your life.
   Yesterday after golf I was at Weidling's for dinner. We played cards up to one o'clock -- I won 9 crowns. Did you have a flirt? Dear, just tell me about your trip, if you were seasick, or the children or nurse Ida.
   Kiss the children from me and say hello to nurse Ida. Olga darling, the time seems to go slower each day, I dread to think that two and a half months are left before you will be home again -- I'm longing dreadfully, why you say -- because you are the best and largest part of me, and if a tree should grow in America, why a leaf of that tree could not live very long on this side (not quite sure of this image, but we know his feelings anyway).
   A big, long sweet warm kiss from your own loving, longing true husband Folke.

OCTOBER 7, 1913

The next day another telegram arrives, this time from Jacksonville, Florida and Folke can relax. But he already worries about the risks involved in motoring.

   He reports of the progress at their new flat. In every letter to Olga, and they are almost daily, he writes lovingly and in great detail how their baby Mary Carita is doing. Could Olga have a better husband? But he has still not had a letter since Olga arrived in America.

October 7, 1913
My own sweet Dearest darling,
I'm full of thanks and joy to know from your telegram that you all Dears are well & home in Jacksonville. The telegram came this morning as a surprise & I can judge from same that you must have taken the train. Did you receive my letter addressed to The Broztell Hotel? Dearest

Own Darling how far you are from me. I'm just longing dreadfully. Take care of yourself and the children, especially when you go motoring. Axel, Sigyn (his brother and wife) Bertil & Ninnie were out last Sunday. The motor went in a ditch and turned over. Bertil fainted for some minutes but all of them came out of it without any harm but dirty and sore all over. Do be careful.

Tell nurse Ida that I have telephoned Engineer Bernson that she had arrived safely to Jacksonville and they were very happy to know it. Give her my best regards.

Yesterday I was quite alone at home with Papa. Can't come in the flat for at least three weeks (their new flat being fixed up). The nurseries and servants rooms are the only ones they have started with and they will be ready this week. The dining room is ready.

Well Darling, Mary Carita is fine and you should certainly be jealous if you could see how Mary Carita smiles and plays with my nose. Today is the first rainy day and cold, so Mary Carita stayed at home. Must close now with love to all, but you Darling, I wished I could give a warm sweet kiss, so also the children.

Your own true loving longing Folke

OCTOBER 8, 1913

The next day Folke writes that as he has received a "wireless letter". I am not quite sure what that meant, but it appears to be something of a letter, and not as short and choppy as a telegram, faster obviously. He was given a promise that Olga and the children who left two weeks before, would return by Christmas, but he is not at all sure that she will. He wants to be reassured.

I have a feeling that Olga in her heart had decided to stay over Christmas before she left, but she could not get her husbands permission to leave with such a prospect, so I believe she decided to soft-pedal it and let him know later. These were different times and women had not got the right to vote and were much more dependent on their husbands both legally and socially.

Folke wonders if the children have forgotten 'their own longing Papa', but how could they possibly have -- they have only been gone for three weeks! To him it seems so much longer.

```
October 8, 1913
Dearest my own Darling Olga,
```
Think today I received your wireless letter which made me happy to know that you had fine weather on your trip over to America. That wireless letter explains to me why you did not send one -- I'll tell you I was very uneasy not receiving any. I didn't understand what had happened. Sometimes I thought you were sick and I did not want to wire. A million kisses back Darling for your thoughtfulness.

Sweetheart, Mary Carita is very well and improving every day in fatness, and all sorts of funny ways. When I come up to her, she is cooing and laughing all over but when I wave goodbye, she doesn't look so pleased at all and begins crying. Then I go back to her and immediately she begins again to smile. Aren't you longing dreadfully to come home to her, your home and to me Darling?

Write me now by return if you have decided to come home before Xmas. A Xmas without you all would make me crazy. My love for you all Dears is strong and true, and I'm sure darling you will please me and come back -- Won't you?

How is Anita and Billy -- my -- our big sweet

angels, hope they haven't forgotten their own longing Papa. Yesterday I was also at home quite alone with Papa and Ruth (his sister). I long for bedtime at early hours to get the day to pass as quickly as possible. Each day is approaching the date when we, sweetheart, meet again. I can burst out crying any minute, I feel lonesome without you but will be a man and with God's help we will all meet before Xmas. Perhaps you get tired to hear that I miss and love you so much but dear I feel so good to speak with you how I feel and what I think. You are the only one who will understand me, my own sweet darling.

Ruth is still at the Avenue (his father's large flat on Avenyn 2, in central Gothenburg). Papa is well and he tries to entertain me all the time and I appreciate it very much, but I prefer to be alone with my thoughts which are with you all my Dear Darlings.

Will you give my best regards to nurse Ida. Hope she is not longing home as hard as I'm longing after you -- the time passes away slower and slower and I hardly dare to think that you shall not be home before Xmas.

Sweetheart, I'm in the new flat every day and my presence is required between 1-3. Two men are up fixing the bathroom, two carpenters put in doors and move closets, two men to put in a water closet, two painters, and then one man who will start putting up the wallpaper. Tomorrow they start with the salon.

Well, must close now with love to your parents, Una, Willie and Bob.

Oceans of kisses to you and to our angels, and last of all, a big long warm kiss and hug from your own true longing hubby
   Folke

OCTOBER 10, 1913

Folke is impressed that they have a new WC (Water Closet) in the new flat. It was only seven years earlier that the city of Gothenburg began connecting water closets to the city sewers. Previously, people used latrines (containers) that were emptied by sanitation workers once a week. It seems very primitive, but it was a hundred years ago and horses were more common in the streets than cars.

As usual, Folke pleads for Olga to come home.

October 10, 1913
My own Dearest Sweet angel,
This is Friday half past seven. I just finished a busy day you know. I want to have a talk with you Dear before I go home.

Well, Mary Carita is fine, healthy and is growing sweeter each day. Today she sat up for 10 minute in her basket. She is soon able to raise herself up. The nurse is very nice and takes very good care of our little angel.

Dearest I long for you all, I don't know why I shall be tortured like this, have I done anything wrong? Dearest own Darling, come home soon with our angels.

The day before yesterday we had the golf meeting. Nothing special at all. Played cards afterwards with Torsten, Orwar and Ivar. Yesterday alone home at the Avenue. I stay alone when you are not at home.

Today I was up in our flat, the W.C is ready for use. Grand isn't it? The bathroom will be ready Tuesday next week. The servants rooms, nurseries and dining room, quite ready.

What are you all doing, take good care of yourself and the children and nurse Ida. This letter will perhaps be in your hand on the 20th of October. The happiest day of my life was when I got you sweet darling as my wife -- a big warm kiss.

Well Darling, give my love to all at 115 East

Adams. Kiss our two angels and take a million kisses from your own true longing, loving hubby Folke

> In the same envelope, there were three pages from a note pad used when keeping scores in connection with playing cards. The handwriting in pencil is very small and neat. On the back it says: "Tear it up when you've read it. It's only for you Dearie"

My Dearest own precious Darling,
I'm sitting all alone in father's smoking room quite alone, nobody at home except the servants. My own fault since Folke Weijdling asked me out boozing but dear sweet little Darling, same does not interest me. <u>You</u> and our sweet angels are my only interest and Darling, I tell you I feel miserable. I long and long after you and feel so lonesome -- You don't know how I feel, somebody has taken out my heart. Can't you come soon? Sweetheart, don't stay too long. My chest is like a lump of lead. My throat full of something hard that makes me feel like crying out. Darling, that's how I feel. Have you not been quite long enough over there? Have you not done your duty Darling?
 Little Mary Carita is so sweet and good and I hope that your longing after her will soon bring you over here. I hate to disturb your nice time over at your parents with my feelings, but Precious, I can't help writing to you how I feel. Tell me frankly if you want these letters or not, but I have nothing else to write. I feel so lonesome. Do you miss me Dear?
 Well Darling, good night and sleep well Dearie. My love to all. Hope nurse Ida is longing home. Mary Carita sends her kisses. Kiss the angels. Warm loving long kiss to you Dearie,

Your own true longing loving Folke

OCTOBER 11, 1913

Folke never forgets to mention Mary Carita in his letters to Olga. I call her by both names as both Folke and Olga use the name "Mary" sometimes and sometimes "Carita" and sometimes "Mary Carita". To avoid confusion, I use both names, Mary Carita, wherever she is referred to. That sweet little baby Mary Carita that gave my grandfather so much comfort and company in 1913, came to be called Mary later in life. My mother and her siblings remembered Mary as much loved and angelic. A gentle and dear sister.

October 11, 1913
My own Dearest Darling,
I'm going out to Hovås in ten minutes with Folke W., but I first want to let you know that little Mary Carita is fine and quite well, touch wood, as they say. I am also well, but feel lonesome and really, to tell the truth, walk about here with no interest at all. Sweetheart, I long dreadfully after you. I think each day is never to come to an end. Yesterday I was also at home quite alone with Ruth. I was and am invited out almost every day, but same interests me no more. I cannot pull together and think you are to be away another two months.

Sweetheart, how are the small angels over in Florida? Hope they are all right. The Janson's have dinner for the Johnson family today. I'm going to that party just to kill time.

Don't mention my feelings to everybody at yours. That's between you and me. My love to you is the strongest and truest you can find.

Dears, a million kisses to you all. Greetings to nurse Ida. Please give my love to your parents, Una, Bob and Willie. When are you coming home? Are you not longing?

Your own loving, longing, true hubby
Folke

OCTOBER 13, 1913
Poor Folke still has not received any letters from Olga, he hopes for letters from New York soon -- with a lot of details about the trip over the Atlantic. If they could have spoken on the phone, how much easier it might have been.

October 13, 1913
My own Dearest Darling Olga,
This is Monday half past 6 and I have finished my work. I have been out to the timber yard and in the flat, but work goes very slow over there. I hope at least they will be ready for us to move in the 1st of November.

Well my sweetheart, how are you getting along and our two angels, I long for you all to come back, can't you come now? There's a big lump in my chest when I sit alone and think of you all, and that is all the time my dear.

Mary Carita is fine and healthy and goes out every day about three hours. We have 4-8 degrees below zero with beautiful hoar frost, but the days are like summer, calm, warm and sunny.

Yesterday was golf, a good sport and a good game, but I won no price. After golf I was at Gösta Dahlman for dinner quite alone, Elsa, Gösta and myself. After dinner we went down to Grand Hotel and had supper there in all simplicity.

Saturday at Janson's was very nice, early home at 11.30 and they asked me to give you their love.

Today, Axel (Folke's brother) went to Copenhagen for business, Ruth and her baby left for Mariero, so now I'm quite alone with Papa. Olga, don't stay longer than you care. Sweetheart, a big long warm kiss. I feel so lonely, I am longing madly after you all. I expect letters tomorrow from New York from you Darling.

Love to all at yours from us all. Kiss and hug the children and keep the best for yourself Darling, my heart, love and kisses in billions
Your own longing true Folke

OCTOBER 14, 1913

Three weeks had passed since Folke left Olga and his children at the railway station in Gothenburg. He already thinks they have been gone long enough as seen from his earlier letters.

A sensitive soul like Folke does not need to read about any more catastrophes on the Atlantic. The memory of the Titanic a year earlier is vivid enough. But the poor man had also read about "The burning of the ship, Volturno" -- a raging and uncontrollable inferno with flames rising eighty feet into the air and clouds of black smoke - described as being "one big furnace, a sea of fire" and "a blazing beacon in the night". Over a hundred passengers lost their lives -- people who travelled on the same ocean his dear wife and children had recently crossed, and would soon cross again. This did not help his nerves. He was already worried about rattle snakes in Florida

October 14, 1913
My own dearest Darling,
This is Tuesday, three weeks since I saw you leaving me quite alone on the station. Sweet darling, I'm longing dreadfully. Mary Carita is sweet and so charming, smiles and gurgles all the time when I play with her. Olga, I tell you the truth that I'm longing for you madly and you must come home for Xmas.

I was all alone at home with Papa yesterday playing patience. Nothing new to say but I want to let you know how we are. Sweetheart, do be careful so about the children for snakes, I read in the Metropolis (a Jacksonville Newspaper that Olga subscribed to in Sweden) that you've got rattle snakes. Do be careful and do not go out for anything risky. I've read the awful accident with the burning Volturno.

Well Dears, I send you millions of kisses and hugs. My love to all at yours. A warm and hearty loving long sweet kiss and hug from your own longing true hubby Folke.

OCTOBER 16, 1913

Finally, Olga's letters from New York arrive. The tone of the letter is very affectionate and she misses Folke a lot.

She and the children and nurse Ida stayed over night at The Broztell Hotel on Fifth Avenue and 27th Street. Olga had expected her parents to meet her and the children, but the parents had already left and instead Olga was met by a family friend, a young man named George Kieferle whom she had not seen for six years. She was quite surprised and pleased to be met and assisted by him. He had no doubt been asked by Olga's parents to take care of Olga and her children and to accompany them on the train and bring them safely down to Jacksonville. It seems a very gentlemanly thing to do. It appears that George has courted Olga's sister Una, and she had not accepted him but Olga writes that he is still very much in love with Una and that he is *"so handsome and such an adorable boy, I do wish so Una had taken him, he'd made such a wonderful brother-in-law."* She writes that he might come back with her to Sweden. Probably to get a chance to meet Una who is supposed to accompany Olga back.

George Kieferle has an automobile and will be able to drive Olga and the children around in Jacksonville. Folke comments that he hopes Olga is not flirting with George.

In this first letter, Olga talks of staying over Xmas and she wants Folke to come over. This alarms Folke as this was against their plans and her promise. On a practical matter, she answers Folke, that yes, her milk stopped just fine and her breasts are soft and she did not have to use the breast pump.

October 16, 1913
My own dearest Darling,
Your two letters posted in New York came to hand this morning and I'm glad to know that George K. took good care of you and followed you to Jacksonville. That was very kind of him. Well Dearie, of course he is welcome here and it's good to have a man to take care of you when going back.

Dearie, your letter about me coming over to spend Xmas is impossible, you know if I should take that holiday I will have none next summer besides it costs a lot of money which we can have for our home and children. I can of course get free from the office if I ask Lundberg to do my work, but I don't like it. I'm sure Papa wouldn't mind, but we shall not think about that. Besides he has nothing really to say, it's my own business if I leave my work. Sweetheart, I thought we had agreed that you would come home to us before Xmas, and your first letter is about wanting to spend Xmas over there.

I enclose a letter with my thoughts, I wrote it yesterday. Tell me frankly, do you intend to stay over Xmas? If you are not coming home, I'm not going to spend Xmas home, I will go to Persia, Russia or England or I do not know where. Darling, I miss you dreadfully, long for you madly. Hope you are not flirting with George.

Well time is up, 7 o clock, so must go home to sit quite alone at Papa's. I kiss the children and send my love to all yours. Greetings to nurse Ida.

Dearie, a million warm sweet kisses and hugs to yourself, your own loving, longing, true hubby Folke

PS: Mary Carita is splendid and is out every day except when the weather is very bad.

OCTOBER 17, 1913
Yesterday Folke received Olga's first letters, the ones from New York, and she has not even written her first letter from Jacksonville yet -- but Folke, who was not prepared for this painful separation, is begging her to come back. Has she not stayed long enough, he keeps asking. Then there is the worrying about Olga and their children running about in autos and being run over by trains and cars. In those days people did not have safety belts and crash bags.

Olga wrote she was surprised how "stout" she has gotten as she had not lost any weight after her third child and writes *"tell your father I'm sorry I may have lost my figure altogether".*

October 17, 1913
My own Dearest Darling,
This is Friday night 7PM and I've just finished a busy day. Darling, my pleasure is then to write to you. Our sweet Mary Carita is fine and is so cunning, but she is missing you. I put her on her stomach and she raises her little head first to the right and then to the left. Dearest, aren't you coming home soon? I'm longing so dreadfully much after you and the children, Dearest, you have no idea. If I had known that absence would be so hard I wouldn't have let you and our sweet angels leave me.

Dearest, our new flat will be nice but work goes slow. The bathroom is now ready and instead of the flat gas stove, we have a round hammered one, looks very nice (probably a gas burner for hot water in the bathroom).

Yesterday, Papa and I went to "Kinne" (the moving pictures) at the Kronan, you know and then we went home. Tonight I'm going home to sit quietly alone longing and longing for you all. Dearest, when you go out, see that no autos or trains run over you, and when you go motoring, don't run too fast, tell them to be careful.

I'm longing to have a letter from Jacksonville. Dearest, I feel awful quite alone from home. My home is with you Dearie. When I go to bed I try to go to sleep at once as I know the next morning will be one day nearer you coming home. Don't let your parents persuade you to stop to Xmas -- well do as you like Dearie -- I think that would kill me.

I am heartbroke. Kisses in billions to you my own darling and the children. <u>My love to all.</u>

Your own loving longing true Folke

OCTOBER 20, 1913

In this letter, Folke looks back on the four years with Olga, the happiest years in his life and he tries to see things more from Olga's point of view. But he still has not received a letter from her in Jacksonville...

October 20, 1913
My Dearest own precious Darling.
I count the days my dear and think today four years ago, how happy I was to get you as my own darling wife. How the day stands clear before me, Dearest. Our four years have been my happiest ones, our good God has blessed us with three lovely healthy children, which we both hope may grow up to Gods and our will. Dear how I wish we could all be together, I miss

you all today more than I can write, my heart is full of thanks for what I've got, but also full of loneliness and sorrow to have you all so far away darlings. You Darling I suppose is enjoying yourself and is having a good time and you deserve it, but Dearie, aren't you longing a little after me and your precious angel Mary Carita?

When I came home for dinner today can you believe darling Mary Carita had a big red rose in her hand to give to her Papa. I wished you could have seen her. She was on nurse Anna's arm and she was so interested in the rose. Sweetheart, I am longing & longing after you. The time seems to be going slower and slower, tomorrow it's four weeks since you left and it seems to me as years.

Darling I see back on the past years, sunny & happy ones but also quarrelling days -- how can we have quarrelled? Can't understand it -- no more, dear.

I have been waiting and waiting for letters from you the last two days but in vain. Today I got a Florida Metropolis (a daily Jacksonville newspaper that Olga subscribed to) dated October 8, and you arrived the 7th, well I hope to get a letter tomorrow. I am longing to hear from you. Dearest darling, can't you telegraph me "Honmiixmas" which will be understood according to our code that you all are well, and coming home for Xmas. Dearest I long to hear from you. Darling, I will answer by wire how we are. Now we are both splendid to health, only that I'm longing, longing dreadfully after you.

Saturday we were all at Victor Janson for dinner and the whole Janson family send you their love. Yesterday I was home for dinner and after golf and Zethraus was also there and Överste Grönwall, and I had to be 4th man for bridge. Played all right but I had rotten luck and lost 12 kronor.

Well Dearie, I wish you all were home -- home to our dear sweet home which isn't quite ready yet but will be I think. How I long to hug our darling Anita and Billy, I suppose they have grown a lot. Have they? Send me a picture of you all. I'll have one taken of Mary Carita this week.
Have you gotten thinner or fatter? What did your father and mother say when you arrived?
Darling, Good Night my own precious own Darling, warm kisses, true ones, a longing hug darling. Kiss our darling children and give our love to your parents and Una, Willie and Bob. Greetings to nurse Ida.
Your own loving, longing, lonesome and true hubby Folke

OCTOBER 22, 1913
Still no letter from Olga in Jacksonville, but he gets some news of Olga through the Jacksonville Newspaper, The Metropolis, from October 8, and he reads a notice in the Social column that Olga and the children have arrived from Sweden to Jacksonville for "a lengthy visit". Folke is disappointed. The newspaper from Jacksonville has managed to arrive in Gothenburg, but no letter from his wife has arrived. He gives Olga the advice to always mail her letters herself so they will not get delayed lying about in someone's pocket.

October 22, 1913
My own Dearest Darling,
Why don't you write me darling. I'm down in the office every day Rydelius brings the mail and I'm always disappointed to know that there is no letter from you. Read yesterday in the Metropolis that you and the children arrived

the day before to Jacksonville for "a lengthy visit."

I'm grieved and anxious about you and my Darlings, longing feeling lonesome. My only pleasure is to have our lovely little Mary Carita with me, she is fine and such a lovely loving little child.

Darling, write me every day, and mail my letters yourself, otherwise they will be carried about in pockets etc., and I will have none. Hope you have got all my letters. Have written you almost every day.

Darling, I kiss you my own little wife, billions warm kisses and so also the children.

Your own true, loving, longing, sad and lonely Folke

OCTOBER 23, 1913

Finally a letter from Olga in Jacksonville. Olga seems preoccupied with the handsome family friend George. Folke is not pleased. I wondered if Olga's comments about George were deliberate to make Folke jealous, but I have decided, that this was probably not the case, or why would she make an innocent comment in another letter, that everyone had gone to bed and she and George were alone in the living room reading and writing letters. At another time, both of them had gone to the Seminole hotel in Jacksonville (The hotel leases the land from Olga's father) to write letters. This is information she would not have divulged, had she had an affair with George. Olga does love Folke very much and those days, "infidelities" came to no more than flirtations. When contraceptives were not available, sex meant pregnancies and Olga and George, who was in love with Olga's sister Una anyway, were no doubt simply good friends.

October 23, 1913
My own Dearest Darling,
Thanks Darling, your first letter from Jacksonville came today this morning and I rushed to my desk to read it. I'm glad you have such a glorious time. Hope that you do not forget us altogether. You don't write anything about Una and Gordon, only <u>George!</u>

Sweetheart, a big kiss, a long one, for your nice letter. Mary Carita and myself are alright but Dearie, longing dreadfully.

Was out with Bertil, Folke, Pelle, and Philip for dinner at Palace Hotel and then oysters at Lorensberg. Had a very nice and gay time. Came home at one. In fact Dearie, I was not tipsy at all, I'm never so jolly as when you are here Darling. Papa is going for dinner today so will be all alone.

Will move over to our flat some day next week. I have been up there today. <u>Our</u> bedroom wallpaper is awfully nice and sweet and Dearie, our flat will be the nicest in Gothenburg when you come home with the children.

I'm, longing dreadfully much after you. Do be careful yourself and the children, when you cross streets, motoring and watch out for snakes at the farm (the Greenfield Plantation recently bought by Olga's father).

Find out Dearie which steamer you intend coming back with. Olga Darling, today is a month since you left me. Oh, I won't go through this again.

Kiss my sweet angels and love to all at yours. Billions of loving kisses and hugs from your own true longing Folke

OCTOBER 27, 1913

Folke feels much abandoned as there has been only one letter from Jacksonville. The new flat is finished and it awaits the lady of the house...Folke urges her to book a steamer right now...

October 27, 1913
My dearest Darling,
You seem to have forgotten your Folke altogether. Now today you have been in Jacksonville 21 days and I've received one letter. Dearie, I write you almost every day, perhaps you don't get them.

Darling Mary Carita and I are all right. I've had a stomach ache but I am quite well now. I'm longing for you Sweetheart, I feel miserable and lonesome, have been home the whole last week at Papa's of course and gone to bed before 10 every night. You see, I wish the days to pass. Some day this week I hope to be able to move in to our flat. They have wall papered all the rooms and what they have left, is to fix up the dining room oak and paint the bathroom. So Clara (the cook) will have to varnish the hard floors and then I will have them put on linoleum. The flat is then ready to receive its "husmor" (Swedish for mistress or housewife) and I hope you will soon come home.

Look up the tourist office and decide on a Cunard steamer Mauretania or Lusitania. If you can get one of those steamers, I will meet you in Liverpool. Do this now sweetheart.

Yesterday Papa and I were for dinner at Zethraeus and then Mr. Herman Petterson, W. Lampe and we played cards at Papa's. I won 8 kronors.

Darling, how are the children? Are they longing for me? Write me all about yourself and you all. My heart is bleeding from missing you all. I's true Dearie.

Love to all -- Billions of kisses and hugs to you.
Your own true longing Folke

OCTOBER 28, 1913
Finally a letter from Olga giving an explanation for not writing:
"Dearest Folke
We've been to the beach every day since my arrival so consequently I've had little time to write but my thoughts are with you night and day. I long to embrace you both and often look at your dear photographs which are on my bureau. The weather has been terribly warm that the only thing we can do is to bathe in the sea..."

But there ought to have been a great deal more letters from her as Folke points out. He is disappointed that she cannot find time to write him.

Folke reports on the almost finished flat and the furniture he has bought for the nursery and he is still waiting for Olga's decision to return soon...

October 28, 1913
Dearest my own Darling,
Thanks sweetheart for your letter telling me you haven't had the time left to write me. I fully understand that you're having such a good time, but darling, spare me at least a few minutes every day and write just only a line. I keep my eyes on the date of posting and between the 10th and the 16th, you didn't write me a letter, only a postcard from the Seminole Hotel (the new and exclusive hotel leased the land from Olga's father for 99 years and the family seems to visit it often). Well Dearie, if you only knew how I'm longing for letters. They are my only <u>pleasure</u> now to look forward to.

Darling, have been to our new flat and now they are soon finished. I have been also at Wesslau (furniture store) and bought a sofa bed for the nurse. It is very nice and it cost 85 kronor with the mattress. I also looked at two wooden beds for our darlings Anita and Billy, a chest of drawers and mirror, a high chest of drawers, a table and chairs, all in white, well also a night table and a lavoir. You will like it I hope. I will go out and look at the linoleum flooring tomorrow. The putting in order of the flat costs pots of money but I do it with pleasure for you my darling. I long long for you all. Now I'm waiting to hear that you've decided to come home soon.

Today we are all going for dinner at 7PM to the Broströms, Papa, Axel, myself, Dans (?), Sigyns, Jacobson, Victor Janson, eighteen people in all.

Perhaps nurse Ida will stay for ever in Jacksonville. Tell her to come home soon with you all. Mary-Carita is so sweet and growing fine, she is lively and so good, sleeps the whole night from 6PM to 7AM and takes her 10 o clock meal sleeping. <u>She</u> is longing for you darling. Love to all from all at home. If <u>you haven't the "time"</u>, ask nurse Ida to write me now and then.

Well darling, I embrace you and send you billions of kisses and also to the children.

Your own true longing loving Folke.

OCTOBER 30, 1913

Folke is happy for Olga's two letters. She can report that she has started "You know" which means her menstruation. She had started to worry about it. A pregnancy was probably not exactly what she had in mind.

I suppose we can "forgive" Olga for not writing for all those days, she is after all a young woman of twenty-three, enjoying herself immensely. She is happy to receive Folke's declarations of love and writes:

"I love you so much, and I'm so glad when the postman comes in the morning with your dear letters --you write

me so lovingly -- do you really (underlined three times) mean all you say? It is perfect to be as happy as we are, are you happy dear? And I certainly appreciate all your thoughtfulness"

In the second letter:
"I'm longing to see the sweet little angel and kiss her warm soft cheeks, she won't know me when I return, the precious baby, but I'll soon let her know I'm her own mama. I wish you were nearer and not separated by such a vast expanse of water. But darling, my mother and father are so happy to have me here that I'm fully repaid for my sacrifice. Our reunion will be all the sweeter -- as the saying goes, 'absence makes the heart grow fonder', is that not true sweetheart?"

October 30, 1913
My own Dearest Darling,
Thanks a million times for your two nice sweet letters and for enclosing some lovely photos, they are indeed sweet, you and our two angels. Billy looks very interesting and Anita I quite understand, she is shy as usual with her little finger in her mouth. I long madly to take you all in my arms, time seems so long and lonesome over here without you. Surely Darling, if you think of me and catch my thoughts you would be occupied day and night. I think of you constantly and it makes me sad when I know you are so far away from me, but my pleasure is to think that we will be together soon and then you mustn't leave me.

Believe me darling that all I write is coming direct from my heart. You ask me Darling if I'm happy, why certainly the happiest man, to have such a loving good wife as you Darling. You know Dearie how I love you, all I live for is for you and our angels, but at present I'm sad to have you all Dears so far away.

Why Dearie, don't brake your promise to come

home for Christmas. You know I would love to come, but sweetheart, let us be sensible and think of the expense and besides, my work in the office would be put back if I left for six weeks. The fixing of the flat cost a lot Darling, new furniture new linoleum, new curtains etc., and what I have added to get the flat in perfect order for you my own Darling.

Mary Carita is so sweet you don't know how. She is so charming when she waves her fingers when I wave my hand. I will take some photos of her. Will also send the music tomorrow when I go to the flat.

Darling, give my love to all. Kiss the angels from me and for yourself a billion kisses, warm long sweet true ones.

Your own longing, loving true hubby Folke.

1913
A NEW APARTMENT

NOVEMBER 1, 1913
This letter is written in their new flat, Berzeliigatan 26, in Gothenburg. People worked Saturdays in those days and Folke has probably come direct from work and he feels lonely in the empty flat...

November 1, 1913
My own Dearest Darling,
This is Saturday afternoon 7.30PM at home in our new flat Dear and I can tell you Dearie that our new home will be sweet when it's ready. Darling, it will be sweetest when you and the children come to it. I long for you more than ever when I sit here alone. Darling, both Mary Carita and myself are all right, she is so cunning and you will not know her when you come and see her. Yes Darling, I give you a kiss from her. I took one for you on her beautiful peach cheeks. We have still fine summer weather and baby is out very much. We've not got any curtains up yet and the dining room floor will be polished (waxed) Monday. On Wednesday we will move in.
    I went down to Almedahls (Linen and textile shop) all by myself this evening to buy curtains for the nursery. Got some lovely thin ones with pink stripes. Darling, tomorrow I will play golf and go for dinner, Bertil and Minnie will

come to Papa.

Sweetheart, my love to all. Kiss my angels from me and Darling, I pray you don't stay too long, we've been separated quite enough. Sweetheart Darling, I love you so much, you are the only one I love.

Billions sweet long warm kisses from your own true loving Folke

NOVEMBER 3, 1913

Folke is asking Olga to commit herself and come home before Christmas. He asks again for that telegram. Olga's mother Anita Dawson, has previously written to Folke thanking him for his sacrifice and asks him to let Olga stay with them over Christmas. After all, she says, Folke will have Olga a lifetime and her parents will only have her for this short time. But Folke informs Olga that he has no answer for her mother.

Folke is truly devoted to Olga and I am not surprised. My grandmother was quite a special person. She was very confident and believed in positive reinforcement and encouragement. She never spoke ill of anyone, she had no need for it, being so self assured. Every relative, her children and grandchildren and friends also thought that they had their own unique relationship with her. She was very much loved and radiated something that drew people to her. She was tremendously charming with a splendid sense of humour and was a great life-force in her family. When she was not there it was profoundly felt.

Men can become "comfortable" when their wives take all the social responsibility and run the home as the project managers they often are, but I doubt Folke was such a man, he was as socially active as Olga. He felt helpless and desperately needed his wife and children back. And the panic set in when he thought they might not be with him for Christmas. He thought two months with her parents was plenty. She had done her duty to her parents certainly. Why might she want to stay away longer?

Folke has asked Olga to send a telegram with their code meaning that she would come home for Christmas. But no such telegram had come.

November 3, 1913
My own Dearest Darling,
Sweetheart, I kiss you a long sweet true kiss for your letter of 20th October. Surely our thoughts met that day.

Well, by now Darling I think you must have got my letter of October 20 and sent me a wire as I asked for. If not, I'll be heartbroken, all my power to keep together without you all Dear will fall to pieces. I wouldn't stand it.

Anyhow, I'll tell you Dear that you should do what you like and consider honest to me, specially as I have sacrificed enough now. My chest is full of tears that want out. I cannot realize that you should be away for Xmas. Two months with your parents is not a short visit and darling I'm sure that when it comes to the end, Una (Olga's sister) is not returning with you. She will not leave her husband, although she is very welcome to us but she can easily leave fourteen days before. Will you thank your mother for her nice letter, but I've no answer to it. You can tell it.

I've today sent an ink stand of iron, it was the only one they had, you must try and get the glass as I dared not send it. Any ashtray was impossible to get, they were sold out, but will get them again about Xmas time. I tried several shops.

I've also sent you the music. Enclosed is a real cheque for 100 kronor for your spending money. Don't forget to buy Helfrid something nice for her expected baby. Don't buy me anything. Buy something for the servants.

Well sweetheart, time is soon 8PM and I am all alone down here (at the office) but will go home to Papa's. Hope my little Billy is all well again, write me particularly hereabout. Mary Carita is quite well and so charming. Can you resist not coming home for Xmas?

Love to all and kiss the babies, but Darling, you have to take billions of true loving warm kisses, long ones, from your sad longing own true Folke.

NOVEMBER 5, 1913

Folke has the new flat nearly ready and he will be moving in soon. He has had to choose and buy many furnishings. And still no telegram from Olga. The uncertainty is unbearable. He fears that if she does not decide to come home now, she might never return. He feels that her parents would happily persuade her to stay for ever...

Olga writes that she has bought two Turkish bath mats and some other equipment for the new bathroom and signs off with a note:
*"Give my love to all and hug my babe tight for me and darling I send you all, everything that is good in me.
Your own true wife Olga"*

November 5, 1913
My own dearest Darling,
This is Mary Carita's 6 months day. She is so cute and loves when I come in to her. Can you stay away so long from her? Darling, I'm sad and only longing for you and the children to come home. I've put the flat quite in order for you all, and then you are so far away that I feel like killing myself.

Sweetheart I know you are in a hard position to leave Jacksonville and your parents, and I know your mother she is strong to persuade you to stop, but Dear Darling, it will be the same thing if you stay over Xmas, then they want you to stay over New Years, then over your birthday (January 10), then for Easter, then for ever if you agreed. Well I'm grieved to have no telegram from you that you are coming home before Xmas. I really thought I could rely more upon your "intention" and took no promise.

Darling, I feel so awfully sad and feel like bursting out in a cry direct from the heart, but still I'm living in the hope that you all Dears will come home soon.

I cannot continue anymore, I only wished I knew for certain that you are coming home sweetheart.

Our flat is now ready and I'm up there twice daily fixing up everything. Will move in Saturday, as tomorrow is Gustavus Adolphus day and I want nurse Anna to be at Papa's in order to see the procession of torches so Friday is not a good day to move so we are waiting until Saturday.

Darling, now kiss the angels and take one from Mary Carita, but from me, take billions warm true kisses direct from my bleeding heart.

My love to all down in Jacksonville.

A long kiss, a warm true one from your own loving longing true hubby Folke

NOVEMBER 6, 1913

Folke mentions Mary Carita, their now 6 months old baby, as often as possible and in great detail to entice Olga to want to go home. He wrote in a previous letter that Mary Carita can almost sit up by herself.

No telegram has arrived - he is heartbroken and tries to avoid friends and relatives in the streets -- when they feel sorry for him, being abandoned by his wife, he feels like crying.

November 6, 1913
My own dearest Darling,
Sweetheart, thanks for your letter concerning our little sweet Mary Carita. You can rest sure that the little angel is very fine and we have a very good nurse in nurse Anna. She takes very good care of the baby. Mary Carita sleeps from 6.30 at night to 7 in the morning, besides 5 hours in the daytime. She is out 3-4 hours except when it's raining.

Do not imagine that Mary Carita sits up for a long time -- sometimes you know our babies have raised themselves up a little, that's what Mary Carita is doing and to rest her back, the nurse puts a cushion under. Call it not sitting up, lying half way up is more correct.

Mary Carita is lying all quite alone almost the whole day and the only time somebody talks to her is in the morning and dinner time. The nurse tells me when Mary Carita needs anything. Darling, are you not longing to come home? How I long for you all, nobody knows but God.

Sweetheart, remember that about mid December, the weather is not so cold as in January and consequently not as dangerous for the children to the change of air. Darling, for this reason I think you better come home as agreed as I do not think it's right of me to leave business, besides I cannot afford it. I will meet you in Liverpool.

Darling, I long dreadfully after you. I feel like a "zero". Today, Bertil and Ninnie, Pelle and Kerstin, Axel and Sigyn and I are going to the Grand Hotel, it is Gustav Adolphus day today.

I miss you so that I begin to feel like running back streets not to meet people since when they pity me, I feel like crying out. The tears certainly come from my heart. Darling, do as you like. My love to all.

No telegram -- I am heartbroken.

Darling kiss my angels and billions long

sweet kisses, warm true ones from your own
loving longing true hubby
   Folke

November 8, 1913

This is moving day to the new flat on Berzeliigatan 26. The building today looks just as it did then in 1913. The flat was very spacious but empty without Olga. Folke had decided to have a dinner for his father the following day which would be Sunday. He no doubt wants to show off the new flat. Olga and Folke had a cook (Clara) in the old flat and it is probably Clara who fixed the food. In those days, men did not cook and wash up as they do now. Food-loving Folke, likes to give the details: soup, turbot (fish), roast beef and Jerusalem artichokes including dessert.

November 8, 1913
My own dearest Darling,
Sweetheart, here in our new flat you have your little daughter Mary Carita and your own longing lonesome hubby. We moved here today at 2 o'clock and indeed, I am glad we are here now.
   I feel lonesome and sad to go round and look at all your things and find no Olga. Darling, you must come home soon. As I told you before Sweetheart, I should certainly like to come and bring you home, but Dearie, I don't consider me to afford it, and besides to make my 2nd trip, to rest up one or two weeks, that is not worth the money which we need for our children and for rainy days and to pay off our villa (the summer-house on the coast called "villa Florida").
   Darling sweetheart, I've just had lunch and 1 hour sleep as I'm invited for dinner at six to Gustav Lundberg together with my father and Mr. Halling. Tomorrow I'm having Papa up for dinner, our first dinner up here, soup, piggvar

(turbot) roast beef, jordärtsskocka (jerusalem artichoke) and dessert.

Darling little Mary Carita is so sweet and she is so fond of me. When I come up to her, she smiles all over and puts her head first to one side and then to the other, laughing and then giving off some funny sounds which I understand to be of joy. I hope Anita and Billy are quite well and how is nurse Ida? Isn't she longing home? I hope she is, perhaps that will bring you home at least a day sooner.

Sweetheart, I think of you day and night and miss you so awfully much. I find no words to explain how miserable I feel, I feel like a dummy.

Give my love to your parents, Una, Bob, Willie and all. Kiss the angels. Una is welcome to sleep in the little nursery. The big nursery is large enough a nurse and three children and if not, Anita and Billy can sleep with us. Fine dear, n'est-ce-pas?

Now Dear, I must dress, a billion warm long sweet true kisses and hugs from your own longing loving true hubby Folke

NOVEMBER 11, 1913

Folke loves food and thinks it important to chronicle what was served for dinner. He tends to do that in his letters throughout his life. It is obvious that the family moved in wealthy circles -- Folke's father was an extremely successful businessman and made many clever property investments in Gothenburg.

November 11, 1913
My own dearest Darling Olga,
This Tuesday and no letter from you Darling since Friday last week, but expect to get one tomorrow. How I long for you all, my only thing in the world. Our little Mary Carita is fine

Darling so lovely and such a loving child. She certainly longs for her Mama.

Saturday last as I told you, we were at Gustav Lundberg and got a very fine dinner. Real Caviar served on a huge piece of ice, a very large piggvar (turbot) and of course soup for starter, then rapphöns (grey Partridge), fresh asparagus, ice cream and fruit. For supper, we got as many oysters we could eat. To drink we had, Mosel wine, Champagne, Claret and Madeira. That was a fine dinner.

On Sunday, Papa was in our new flat and I served a good dinner. For supper, Helfrid and Folke came up and Clara (the cook) gave us sweetbread, a good mayonnaise salad of shrimps and salad and cold roast beef with fried potatoes. They thought we had got a very much nicer flat now, without comparison.

Yesterday I was quite alone for supper. Papa came up for dinner, cold roast beef, as we had been out to mother's grave it being their wedding day.

Today is the yearly Goose Day Celebration and I'll go for dinner to Bertil at seven. He invited me first, then Folke rang and invited me for goose and when I told Papa he said, "When shall we eat our goose at home?"

Well, this is all what I've done since last letter. Darling, I hope soon to have news from you, good news. Sweetheart, I long for you dreadfully and the days pass off slower and slower.

Kiss my, our, two darling children and Darling to you I send billions warm long kisses.

Your own longing, loving, sad, true hubby
Folke

NOVEMBER 13, 1913

Folke still hopes for Olga's return before Christmas. There is a tug of war between Folke and Olga's parents who wish her to stay. It is up to Olga, he replies while he simultaneously writes to Olga and pleads with her.

Olga's father died unexpectedly two years later in 1916 and she was unable to go home during his illness -- the First World War was on and no one could travel on a steamer until it was over in 1918.

But lonesome and longing Folke, sitting in the smoking room writing his letter to Olga on November 13, 1913, knew only one thing -- that he had been alone far too long, that he had sacrificed himself long enough and that he simply wanted his wife and children to come home. Or his heart would burst.

I think that my 27 year old grandfather was very sensible to leave the decision to Olga herself and not to "force" her as another man might have tried to do. I find this letter sensible and mature for such a young man. This letter is more varied than any other previously and he goes into the subject of his utter fidelity to his Olga.

November 13, 1913
My own dearest Darling Olga,
Today, this morning, I got two letters from you. That explains why I had to wait a whole long week. Thanks sweetheart, they make me so happy and to know that you all are well. You see Darling, Your longing hubby has no other pleasure than to wait and long for letters from you.

Now to the worst part of the whole trip, the returning subject. You must understand Darling that I'm quite alone here, except for little Mary Carita which of course is a great joy and relief in my loneliness, but you cannot count her as company now for the coming Xmas. Sweetheart, you will then find me all alone for Xmas after a long dreadful separation which you Darling must admit was a sacrifice, in fact, the biggest sacrifice I could make, to let my own Darling wife and our children leave me.

Darling, you must, and your parents ought to think the same and willingly let you go home. Darling, I quite understand that you will give them such a great pleasure to stay over Xmas, but Dearie, I see it this way, that you have stayed with them over two months and a few days longer counts not so much for them as for me, having only lived in the hope that you and our darling children should come home and spend Xmas all together. You say that perhaps it will be the last Xmas you will spend with your parents, very well, it can be the last Xmas we spend together. Nobody knows except our Good God.

Sweetheart, I've told you how I feel and want to tell you that have you any proposal what I shall do during the long Xmas and New Year holidays? Well I don't know. I feel like my heart should burst. I do not know where I should go as I do not feel, or do not think me able to spend Xmas in any of my relations home without you. It would make me miserable to think back on the years we have been together and not being together now.

I'm sure you feel like coming home and spend Xmas at home here with your own family. Now sweetheart, I've told you plainly what I think and how I feel, I have not said yes, have not sad no. I leave it all with you dear, do which you consider right. I think you that you would have had much more out of the trip if you had decided something and not having that constantly on your brain -- shall I go home or not.

Well Darling, I'll let you know now that if you intend going home before Xmas, you can take either:
Kaiserin Augustin Victoria (Hamburg America Line) on December 11, which arrives Hamburg on

December 20
or
Coronia (Cunard Line) on December 13, which arrives Liverpool on December 20
or
Olympic (Cunard Line) on December 13, which arrives Southhampton on December 20.

Now Dear Darling, believe me I cried a good deal just when I wrote about the boats as I'm fairly sure that I've done it unnecessarily. Anyhow Dear, what I do for you is done out of love and there can never be too much love. Decide now for your own, and use the code if you are coming for instance, if you take Kaiserin Augustin Victoria, telegraph "Jupgeedhoe Victoria" or if you take the Coronia, telegraph "jupgeedhyf Coronia" or if any of the other steamers, just telegraph the date and name.

I expect a telegram if you decide to remain, please wire "honmilater" and I will understand that "later" means that you are not coming home for Christmas. I hope that I'll not receive such a wire.

Now dear, I will meet you in Liverpool, Southhampton or Hamburg whatever you decide. If they tell you that the Hamburg America Line has a steamer, take that line as you and the children will not have to change anywhere. But Darling don't take any smaller boat than 18,000 tons, it's too rough to go winter time on such a small boat.

Your parents can come next Xmas and spend some time with us. Now about Una. Of course she is <u>very welcome</u> and I repeat my former letter that I consider she can leave Gordon for Xmas <u>just as well as you can stay away from your longing Folke</u>. Can't Gordon come along and stay. A months, six weeks holiday is not too much for him working so hard.

Darling Sweetheart, I long dreadfully after

you, I'm sitting all alone in the smoking room and my eyes are full of tears, I've had enough of this constantly alone, alone, alone, alone.

Darling, our Angel Mary Carita is so fine and good, she gains one hekto a week and nurse Anna takes her up to Miss Källander every week and she thinks she is a very fine child. Touch wood.

I'm doing nothing of the kind Dear, you know Dear what I mean, I'm true as gold, and to give myself to another would ruin my love to you altogether. My character is far better than to go and spoil my life. There is no promise holding me back, only my heart telling me that I'm only your own little "baby" and nobody else's.

The day before yesterday I was at Bertil's for goose and we three played bridge afterwards. Sweetheart, yesterday I was home alone, tonight home alone. After work I often go to the moving pictures, sometimes with Papa, but mostly quite alone, alone.

Clara and Hildur (the servants) have worked hard and are taking good care of me. Write them a postcard.

Sweetheart, I certainly want a telegram from you in reply to this letter, whether it will make me happy or heartbroken. I hope you don't find the separation so hard as I feel. If I'd known how hard, I would never have let you go. Tell your parents that for them the Xmas will surely be joyful in any case getting Willie home for Xmas.

Sweetheart, do what your heart tells you. You have fulfilled your promise to spend some time in Jacksonville. Kiss my two loving children Anita and Billy. Mary Carita kisses you.

Darling, a billion sweet good night kisses from your own loving longing sad true hubby Folke

NOVEMBER 13, 1913
The same evening, Folke also writes to Olga's parents. I thought his tactic very clever, to leave it all to Olga.

November 13, 1913
My Dear Mama and Papa,
I'm sure you hear from Olga all about Mary Carita and me here at home. I'm thankful to you both for the nice time you are giving Olga by inviting her and our two children over.

Of course I know that you all wish to have your daughter over Xmas, but you don't know how dreadfully lonesome I feel and how hard the separation is. Olga is everything for me, and an extension of her visit in Jacksonville over Xmas would make it much harder for me.

If I was a man fond of outdoor life I'm sure I would not mind her staying, but a man loving his wife, his children and his home, it's very hard indeed and I hope you will not miss her too much if she leaves before Xmas.

We are always happy to see you here and I think it would be nice if you could come over to our new home and spend Xmas another year as I believe it is impossible now when your house is being built.

Pardon me for not having written before thanking you for the nice birthday present. Thanks also for your letter. But I have no answer. Olga will answer, and I pray that she will hold to her promise as I held to mine, in not objecting to her and the children going to see you-- and her to come home for Xmas.

My very best love and kisses to you, Olga, the children, Una and Bob, Willie and all.
  I'm your affectionate son-in-law
  Folke

NOVEMBER 18, 1913
Olga probably enjoys Folke's social gossip in this letter. The scandal of the day was that the Swedish prince Wilhelm who had married Grand Duchess Maria Pavlovna of Russia in 1908, was now planning to be divorced.

Folke also speaks of a "props meeting" at the Palace Hotel and that must have been a business matter regarding props (wooden supports) for British coal mines, a large export item for the family business. There was an organization called "The Swedish Pitprops-Exporters' Association" and it was probably a meeting with them he referred to.

And the old battle to convince Olga to come home continues. Certainly no man has ever pleaded more for his wife to return than Folke, these last months. Will he succeed when Olga writes thus?

"Well my darling little boy, there's no more news, only I miss you and long to embrace you. This separation will make us appreciate each other all the more, we became so estranged this summer so I think the separation was intended by fate.

Good night, sleep well and dream of me, sweet precious little boy"

November 18, 1913
My own dearest Darling,
No letter since Saturday and this is Tuesday but I expect one tomorrow full of good news that you all my Dears are returning before Xmas. Aime's have been in Paris with their baby but is coming home tomorrow. Sweetheart Darling, you must come home for Xmas. I feel miserable and downhearted. Everything seems so sad and lonesome. Mary Carita is so sweet but I should think you would want to come home and hug her.
Now to some scandals. Prince Wilhelm and Maria are definitely going to be divorced. Oswald Westerbergs are divorced but perhaps

I've written you that before. Putte Helling who was going to marry soon went on a business trip to Paris, met some cardsharpers and lost 700 kronors for his firm, came home and was sorry that his willpower was so weak, so he postponed the wedding and has left for America again to try himself once more.

Tomorrow we are all invited for dinner to Herbert Jacobson and today we have a props meeting at Palace Hotel.

Saturday I had a very good dinner at Folke's and although there was a fine "maskerad bal" (costume ball) at the concert, I didn't go. Nothing like that interests me when you Dear is not with me. Sunday I played golf with Folke W. and I had dinner afterwards at Papa's.

Have just phoned Carlströms and Thyra, Astrid and Gunhild, all of them have been very sick with inflammation of the lungs but are now getting better.

Darling, my own little Olga, kiss my own angels and do please come home for Xmas.

Kisses in billions to you and a big hug from your own longing loving true hubby

Folke. Love to all

NOVEMBER 20, 1913

Folke says he will say no more regarding Olga returning before Christmas, only to return to the subject later in the letter. He reports in great detail of Mary Carita's weight and general condition, no doubt to make Olga long for her, but generally, Folke liked to provide details of this kind in his letters which make them interesting to read today. Sometimes I wonder when I see his beautifully written letters, so full of details, if he ever thought of posterity when he wrote them. But it was probably just his nature to be interested in things, and to want to share things with others. I like how considerate he was of the servants, he asked Olga in a previous letter to write a postcard to them and to bring them Christmas gifts when she returned and not to buy any for him.

November 20, 1913
My own Dearest Darling,
Having waited and longed for several days I received two letters this morning from you Darling and they made me so happy and the photos of you are very fine. I haven't taken one of the baby yet. The weather is is so unreliable now, so cannot arrange anything. Did you take both cameras?

Darling, I'm not going to write more about you coming home before Xmas. You know how I feel. Miserable if you do not come.

Truly dear, our little Mary Carita is fine and her flesh is very firm. She weighed 7 kilos (15.4 lbs) yesterday, gained 150 grams last week. She hasn't any teeth yet.

Was at Herbert Jacobson yesterday and had a nice time. We have had an awful storm for the last two days with lots of rain.

Sweetheart Darling, we shall not alter our baby's name. Anita is written as "Ragnhild Anita" so I think we shall keep the names as they are, "Mary Carita".

My little stomach is in an awful state for the last days, pains and diarrhea, but I have only had light food today so hope to get well for tomorrow when we are having Hakon Leffler's "svensexa" (bachelor's party). Well Sweetheart, I feel awfully down. Kiss the two darling children and to you I send millions of hugs and kisses, warm loving ones. Give my love to all at yours.

Darling, I long dreadfully after you, I'm counting the days and if you stay over Xmas, that means two months more of not "only" one month which is quite enough if you don't want

to kill me.
   Good night sweet Darling and a hug and kiss, your own true loving longing hubby
   Folke

NOVEMBER 22, 1913

The weather is till warm in Florida and Olga writes how they all walk around in white dresses. They have fished up some lovely oysters on the beach and roasted them and Olga has tried to dance the "Turkey Trot" and the new popular dance called "Tango" but she "made a mess of it" and she hopes Folke will teach her when she comes home.

On that old subject of coming home, Olga writes: *"....Your letter in Swedish came this morning and I enjoyed it immensely, especially all the nice things you said. Now darling, stick it out until January and we will be new married again and love each other all the more. I long madly for you both but think that when I have gone so far, I might just as well spend Xmas here and be done with it -- you understand don't you Darling? And I'm sure God will bless you for your unselfishness*
   Love from your loving Olga"

November 22, 1913
My own Dearest Darling Olga,
Thanks sweetheart for your letter November 9, which I received this morning. You do not know how happy your letters make me. I only wished that you will soon be home. You say darling, "be a man", but you wouldn't say that again if you know how hard and sad it is for me to be alone here, day after day. By now I suppose you will soon receive my letter telling you that I'm expecting you home, but I'm trying to put myself into that you are staying over, but that is impossible. I don't think you would.

Darling, our little Mary Carita is so darling I certainly think you will get crazy in her when you return. She is quite well, touch wood. Have just finished my dinner all alone, chicken with rice and one of Clara's cakes. You see, this is Saturday evening and I've been playing golf. The air was so lovely today, the first day since last Sunday.

Darling Sweetheart, I love you so much and think sweetheart, that we will have a honeymoon all our life in our new sweet home. Yes think Darling of me and come home! Darling, I go about in the flat and look round for you and Darling, I find you nowhere, but surely you are with me in my heart and in my thoughts.

Precious Darling, I long so much after you and do not know how to kill time. Darling sweetheart I'm longing dreadfully and it is so hard not to have you and the babies. Had I lots of money, I would come direct to you. Now about Una (Olga's sister) frankly she is very welcome to our sweet home, but I think she might be able to leave fourteen days earlier and not go with you on the 11th of December.

Darling, you see now when you have stayed so long over in Jacksonville, it's not so hard for your parents to let you go home to me, having gone here in Sweden, heartbroken, with a bleeding heart and longing and longing. Darling own sweetheart, do come home I beg you.

You know Elsa Ewert, engaged to Gadd, died the other day.

Papa is quite well, will come home to me for dinner tomorrow and I have asked Bertil as Ninnie is in Stockholm for fourteen days. Orwar will also come.

Hakou's wedding will be on Thursday next week and Bertil, Folke W., Axel, Sigyn, Pelle and Kerstin, Arnold all are going up to Uppsala. I've said no as I want to go and meet you in

Bremen? or Liverpool? or Hamburg and to go up there (to Uppsala) without you is not worth the money.

Now sweet Darling Olga my own little wife, a warm hug and a sweet good night kiss. You will find the flat very nice I hope and dear, your bed stands empty, and empty all the time. I nearly get lost in our big bedroom.

Helfrid hasn't got any baby yet but it is expected any day. I have given Hildur (one of the servants) fourteen days free to go home to hers.

Darling don't buy me anything. I do not want anything except You and the babies to come home for Xmas. Gold or Diamonds would not be worth anything comparing to you and babies coming home. That's all I wish.

Kiss our angels and a soft sweet kiss from your little Mary Carita and I send you millions kisses and warm hugs.

Your own loving, longing true hubby
Folke. Love to all

NOVEMBER 25, 1913

Olga has just received his letter dated November 6, which obviously has touched her deeply and writes..

"You see my darling I cannot leave before Xmas, I feel it my duty to see Willie (her brother who was due to come home for Xmas) and spend <u>one</u> Xmas with my parents although it would be a million times much nicer to be home with <u>you</u> (underlined three times) and Mary Carita. My own sweet boy, if you only knew how much I long for you and sometimes I feel as if I'd go crazy, but we must both have patience and then <u>forever</u> and <u>forever</u> be together. So stick it out. God will <u>surely</u> bless us for this sacrifice, we must not be <u>too</u> selfish....

Anita is beginning to speak English so well, every day she says something new, you darling will be surprised to see them, they both have grown so and Anita is so old in her ways. People here are wild about them and do you know why they are so fine and healthy dear -- because you are so clean pure and good, so God has blessed our offspring.

A long sweet kiss from your loving Olga - forever and forever yours"

November 25, 1913
My own dearest Darling little wife,
Thanks darling sweetheart for your letter which I received yesterday, and I'm now going to answer the questions.

As I told you before, Hildur (one of the servants) is away for a fortnight as Clara (the cook) will start at the Palace Hotel later on.

The carriage soufflet has been reconditioned long ago.

My own dearest Darling, I expect this will be my last letter to Jacksonville as I'm in the hope that you will come home before Xmas and I'm now expecting a cable from you any minute that you have decided to return. I pray to God that he will give you the strength to cable me the happy news as I think that I have had enough torture.

I dread to think of being alone over Xmas and New Year from my own loving wife and children, Oh Olga dear, you do not know how I dread it and how I'm thinking of it Sweetheart. I'm taken good care of by everyone and my father tries to cheer me up, but Dear, when I come alone, my eyes get wet and I'm thinking, what bad have I done to be left so lonely.

Well, when you receive this letter I hope you will be just about to leave for New York and I'll meet you on this side. How glad I will be.

Must close now with billions of kisses to the children and you Darling, a warm long soft loving kiss and hug from your own longing loving true hubby Folke

PS:
Was at the Vaudeville yesterday with Papa and a businessman and afterwards at Lorensberg, had oysters and champagne. Will now go to Golf meeting at Palace.
Love to all.
   Oh Dear!   WELCOME HOME

DECEMBER 3, 1913
Folke has expected a telegram with the "happy news". He has been prepared to travel to any of the ports, Liverpool, Hamburg or Strasbourg, to meet up with his family. As a matter of fact, he did not receive any cable at all, so he telegraphed Olga and from her answer he understood that she was not coming back.

"Darling Folke,
Your cable came at dinner time and caused quite a confusion, mama got so anxious but I just knew what it was. Well, I have cabled "homilater" and know that it will make you sad, but darling I've told you why in my previous letters -- next month we will meet, it almost seems too good to be true and how grand it will be to come home to my own new home, everything clean and fresh and to you and Mary Carita."

Olga had prepared Folke for her decision to stay, but never said it firmly until now, probably out of consideration for him. So how did poor Folke handle this? He had told Olga in previous letters that it would kill him if she did no come home.

Folke did not die, of course, but he was beside himself with loneliness and he had developed a nervous stomach condition due to the stress. This illness had brought matters to a head and the family doctor intervened and told Folke straight out what he had to do.

December 3, 1913
My own Dearest Darling,
The last letter I wrote you darling is about a week ago and I have not written you thinking I should get a cable that you all were coming for Xmas. When I did not receive any cable I cabled you and could understand from your answer that you were going to stay in Jacksonville over Christmas and not return until January.

Darling, you see after I wrote you that last letter I got very ill in my stomach and feared I'd gotten appendicitis, but got relieved when Dr. Ström came up and told me that it wasn't appendicitis, but that I had to rest in bed fore some days and live on milk and a soup made from oats, as he told me I'd nervous stomach dyspepsia. He asked me if you were coming home for Xmas and I told him that you were not coming home. He told me that I had better go over and bring you home, as to be alone the coming Xmas would not make my nervous dyspepsia any better, on the contrary.

You, dear Darling must know that I have struggled hard to pull together, but my anxiety for you all has not been good for me. I cannot help that I love you and long so much after you, my Dear wife and children. You don't know Dear, how I have tried the time to pass quickly, but my thoughts have constantly been over in Jacksonville for you all my Dears, but the approaching Xmas holidays and thus the worry about you on the boat etc., have made me nervous. I'm now better in my stomach but must be careful with what I eat.

I quite agree with you darling that it is an unnecessary expense to cross the Atlantic for such a short time and this payment is really an unexpected one as I had calculated to save up two or three thousand kronors this year and pay off on our villa (villa Florida their summer house on the coast at Särö) but now all will go but Darling, you think the same as I'm sure, that the health goes before anything and when Dr. Ström even had written to my father as enclosed, I decided to leave rather than cable for you telling that I was ill, which would have worried you.

I cannot and will not ask my father to pay my way this time, also I know he has got lots of money to pay now when Axel (Folke's brother) marries and Rolf also (Folke's other brother) and then Ruth (Folke's sister) and then Frej (another of Folke's brothers).

Now, about our little Mary Carita, she is fine and growing big. Darling, she is so sweet and I feel bad to leave her, she almost says "Papa". Dr. Ström looked at her and he's promised to come up and see about her, and if anything the slightest with Mary Carita, he told me the servants can only telephone him and he will come up immediately. I will have her photographed so I can bring some with me.

I'm leaving Monday or Tuesday next week over land to Liverpool and will take the Lusitania the 13th December from Liverpool, expected in New York the 18th when I will take the first train for Jacksonville. If necessary to call at any hotel it will be Broztell (The same New York hotel used by Olga and her family)

Long to have you Darling and my children in my arms. Lundberg (at the office) is away all this week so have enough business to think of.

Kiss my darlings and billions to you and hugs.
Love to all.
Your longing own longing true hubby Folke
PS:
First of all, thank your parents that I'm welcome and then Dear explain to them the reason why I'm coming over -- I have not the time to write to them.

Folke was booked on the British owned Lusitania which, when it was launched in 1906, had been the largest ship in the world. We all know what happened to the Lusitania -- it was torpedoed in 1915 by a German submarine during the First World War. So Folke was secure on this trip in 1913. The war started in 1914.

After this letter, there are suddenly no more letters for us to read and I feel strange because I would have liked to know what happened when Folke arrived in Florida, how his trip went, which boat they chose for their return trip and what Olga thought when she saw her baby Mary Carita after four months absence. And of course, what Olga thought of the newly furnished flat. But there are no letters or documents left behind to give us those answers -- finding anything is like staring into a black void. But perhaps that is as it should be. Folke was no longer unhappy and had no need to write a letter every other day. He had his Olga and his children. He spent his time with them enjoying life instead of writing lonely letters to Olga on a different continent.

***

What took place in Folke and Olga's life in 1913, became an intense reality for me as I got closely involved in their lives reading and typing their correspondence. This brief window in Olga and Folke's long life, magically opened up more than a hundred years later through grandfather Folke's letters and his deep longing for his darling wife -- and for grandmother Olga loving and saving them. I received them in my hands, after my mother died, in neat little bundles tied with different coloured ribbons. Thank you grandmother Olga!

I think of all the time we spend every day, writing an enormous volume of words in emails and Twitters, words that will be gone as fast as they are written-- unless someone prints them and puts them in a file and makes a conscious effort to save them generation after generation, but how often does that happen? Are they even worth preserving? How well are they crafted?

Will anyone be able to map my or your feelings a hundred years from now -- will there be anything left behind, like Folke's finely crafted letters, so expertly written? And so moving?

1925
FOLKE AT LYSHOLMEN
OLGA IN BRUSSELS

Olga and Folke, safe from the conflict of war in neutral Sweden, continued having children and Folke and his father made large profits from wood exports to Britain, and considering these unexpected profits, the opportunity to build a large and impressive house on the ocean could not have been more favourable for the young couple.

Folke had selected a barren peninsula on Särö for the new house, not quite where most of the posh people lived, in the very heart of the fashionable seaside resort, Särö, on the Swedish West coast.

The peninsula Folke had chosen would provide a grand, more secluded and spacious setting for Olga and Folke's new home.

Olga had been shocked when she first saw what Folke proposed for their new home, on a bare rock on a peninsula -- could one really build a house there? But Folke's enthusiasm was catching and when the house was finished in 1918, it had many wide terraces built from local river stones, all filled with soil and planted with trees. Very soon this barren peninsula would be green indeed.

This impressive three story house on the ocean was to remain their residence for the rest of their lives. It was the perfect home for the couple and their nine children.

There are no letters from Folke to Olga until 1925 when Olga travelled to Brussels and 1926 when she went to Florida to visit her sick mother. He wrote to her from their home Lysholmen, keeping Olga informed about the life in the large house and its many inhabitants.

MARCH 14, 1925

Olga left Sweden in March 1925 with her close friend Joy Bratt to meet up with Olga's mother Anita Ball in Brussels. Together they spent a few weeks travelling. Folke mentioned in a letter that Olga needed a rest probably after some illness.

Folke never stopped smoking as Olga had hoped when they were engaged, and he often suffered from bronchitis -- as when he wrote this letter. Their son Bo-Erling's birthday is coming up and Folke tells Olga what clothes he has bought for him. Most men at that time would leave all those things to their wife, but Folke got closely involved with his children, shopping and caring for them.

It is obvious that Olga went away rather suddenly with her friend Joy Bratt, to meet with Olga's mother who was in Brussels with Willie, Olga's younger brother. Folke probably feels low being home sick and without Olga and the letter reflects it. As we have seen before, Folke is emotionally dependent on her.

```
March 14, 1925
My Dearest Darling,
Here I'm again and wish to thank you for your
letter which I got forwarded from the office.
I've been feeling lonely all day and been in bed
until half past 12. I'm feeling the same, but
it is not one of the usual bronchitis I have.
    For Bo-Erling, Alma (the cook) is making a
```

walnut cake and I have bought him three pairs of stockings, one pair of mittens, one pair of brown boots with rubber soles, one pair of lackskor (patent leather shoes) and some small toys as well. He does not want anything else but clothes.

Hope you found Mama all right and that she will accompany you here. If you dread the boat, take the train my Dear.

Well you can understand that I've nothing more to say when I've seen nobody and talked to nobody. The children are luckily fine and healthy looking.

Well I hope you will have a nice time and soon come home with fresh nerves, restored from your "selfish Folke".

My Dear, I feel like I would want to go away and hide myself in a big forest, away from everybody except you.

Give my love to Mama and for yourself, the children send you big kisses. Darling Olga, take a big hug and a long kiss from your own devoted and longing
Folke

MARCH 17, 1925

Olga and Folke discuss in their letters whether Olga's mother should return with her to Sweden or not. Folke says that she is always welcome. But unfortunately she did not return with Olga to Sweden. If only Olga had brought her mother back with her in 1925 when her mother could still travel, then Olga would have been spared much hardship having to travel to her mother's bedside in 1926 and 1931 (her mother died in 1931).

Folke had a lot of work to do and on top of everything he worried about a lockout and a general strike that might hit their sawmill.

Folke had to put up being separated from Olga again. He thought that perhaps he loved her too much. More than she loved him...?

March 17, 1925
My own dearest Darling Olga,
Thanks for your letters received yesterday and today. From same I cannot understand anything yet of your plans. You do not mention anything. W. Bratt (husband of Olga's travelling companion, Joy) has telephoned me nearly every day and today he informed me that you and Mama intend leaving for Paris.

Well, let me know your plans and perhaps this letter will not even reach you before leaving. W. Bratt was worried what should become of Joy, but I said that I'm sure all will go well.

The children at home are quite well and I'm a little better. Was at doctor Ström yesterday and he has examined my lungs and they are all right.

I went with Mr. and Mrs. Gustaf Lundberg yesterday at 6PM to Harald Wennerberg and there was Mrs. Elsa Schwartz and one Stockholm man, W.Lindgren. Had a nice game of bridge. Stopped overnight with Papa, and he tried to do all he could to get my room warm and also the bed. He even put two ordinary bottles with hot water in my bed, so when I went to bed, it was warm, but also wet; -- he had put in the corks too loose so I had to redo the whole bed. Slept bad at night, dreaming of you all the time.

God knows I feel miserable and time goes awfully slow. I feel like a schoolboy who longs for a holiday which never comes. I hate to be separated like this, but it is your wish and what can I do. Let me know darling, your plans. Can't you get Mama with you over here.

Last night we had some snow but it is much warmer today and the snow is gradually going away.

Today is a club meeting with dinner at 7PM, they want me to join but I really have not the feeling to go but I might change my mind. My business takes all my brain to keep everything together, and on top of everything, there is a lockout involving 130,000 workers, among all sawmills, textile mills and verkstadsarbetare (workshop workers). Our mill is not in it yet, but the workmen federation (union) is discussing the matter and they may answer back with a general strike.

Well, Bo-Erling was very pleased with his birthday and I made a speech for him and we all said "hurrahs" for him as well as I could with my bad throat. Then we sang "Ja Må Han Leva" etc. (Happy Birthday etc).

Bertil Wijk came up on Sunday and sat down with me in the radio room (at the office) and I got in Holland splendidly at 1PM. Then we also heard the weather reports. He thought the radio was very good.

Darling, now I must finish with many long kisses and hope you will soon begin to feel homesick and return to your loving hubby, who perhaps loves you too much. Do I? I wish you loved me half as much.

A big and a long kiss from your devoted
Folke.
Love to Mama

MARCH 18, 1925

Later in this letter, Folke is proud to tell Olga of how he came upon a treasure trove of ice. In 1925, the modern electric refrigerator had not come into general use in Sweden and people still depended upon ice-boxes. A large block of ice was placed in the top compartment of the icebox and as the ice melted slowly, it dripped into a container below and this process kept the food cold.

It was important to have access to ice and in cities, there were ice deliveries, men who carried large blocks of ice with a pair of tongues and delivered them into your ice box. In the country, people had to get the ice from the sea or a lake and then store it in an ice-house where the ice, covered with masses of saw dust was preserved from winter to winter, when they would stock up on new ice again.

March 18, 1925
Villa Lysholmen, Släp
My Dearest Darling Olga,
Here I am again out at the house and the children I found rosy and fine. The frost has turned into the most lovely spring weather with bright sunshine.

I came out in the car which has been for repairs for the usual wheel troubles. I hope it won't come back.

I decided to go to the club meeting and had a good game of bridge with Carl Lyon, Nils Norling, Dr. Tehrödl (?). Among others there were Eric, Philip, Axel, Metcalfe, Annulf Olsson, Ahrenberg, Pelle Söderberg, Knuckenberg, Pelle Hertz, in all 22.

I came home at 2.15 in the morning and had to sit and talk with Papa until 3.10. He has the bad habit of lying awake all night until I come home.

When I came home to dress in the flat, Papa was down at Allers and would you believe he had "Les trois grace" (the three graces) for dinner there, Augusta Lindström, Clara Bergman and Ellen Waroden(?) and they all came up at 6 and had coffee and Benedictine liqueur.

Papa had invited Augusta L. and Clara B. to the Victoria as Ellen Waroden was going there. Tant Clara sends her heartiest love to you and hoped that you would gain a lot in strength while away. She also told me she had hoped to see you longer the day you left.

Well Darling, I feel awfully lonely. I wished you could come round me and just lay your soft arms around my shoulders, but you have run away from me. That trip of yours came to be decided I think too quick.

I can tell you that we have had enough cold weather just to get some ice on Wijk's pond. When I spoke with Bertil Wijk this morning on the phone, he told me that I could take the rest if there was any. Generous offer, so I asked Adolf (the gardener) to go and have a look. He phoned me att 11AM that there was no ice whatever to get, but that we could get ice in our usual place, you know the small river between Släp and Mrs. Weijdling.

Adolf got Hjalmar and Fritz for 5 hours and they got 100 pieces 5 inches thick ice, much nicer ice than Wijk's, so when I came out at 4PM, I met them and paid them 10 kronors in all. Tomorrow I have rented a horse and carriage to take the ice to the icehouse. It was quite as if I had found, a treasure.

I'm still hoarse, but better. Will continue this letter tomorrow as the ink is running out (the ink is considerably weaker on the paper). Good night sweet Darling, and a big hug and a long kiss from your own longing, loving hubby Folke.

Tuesday office (the ink strong again)
I was in the hope of receiving a letter today as I did not get any yesterday, but was greatly disappointed. Well darling, nothing new since last night. Lovely spring weather and the thrushes have arrived now.

Hope to hear from you Sweetheart. I feel so lonely.
Your own loving hubby
Folke

1926
SICKBED IN FLORIDA

Early in 1926, Olga's sister Una sent a telegram to Olga asking her to come home because their mother Anita Dawson was very ill. Olga and Folke had eight children at this time and Folke was not happy to see his wife leave him. He knew that Olga might be gone for many months -- her absence this time turned out to be over three monthss. Olga's mother was indeed very ill and needed her daughter in more ways than one as it turned out.

Olga spent the days by her mother's bedside and as she wrote to Folke *"it is very warm here and I have very little energy and just sit with Mama all day long. She has many people who visit her and are kind and sweet. Her sister who is a Catholic nun is here staying with us. We wrote for her to come, she is the only sister left and Mama expressed a desire to have her come down. I was surprised when she told us she could remain as long as she liked, she is most entertaining and jolly and very witty. Today she spent the day with Willie to look all over Jacksonville in his Ford.*

....Folke, do you know, it is awfully difficult for me to leave Mama in her weak condition, Mama may not live long and I would never forgive myself if I left her just now."

Olga was thirty-six and did not have any

experience sitting by a close relative's sick or death-bed. Olga's father had died when she was only 26 during World War 1, and at that time, as mentioned, she could not travel home. So one well understands that seeing her mother so ill had quite stunned and shocked her. Having lived with my grandmother, Olga, for many months at various times when I was in my teens and later, I think I can say she was the kind of person who kept the pain to herself and her letter writing to a minimum when it came to this subject.

MARCH 22, 1926

Folke had been in England on a business trip during all of March. This is one of many of the letters he sent almost every day from England. He had sold many consignments of "laths", the thin strips of wood used to make interior walls and ceilings. This one item had made Folke and his father quite prosperous over the years. They manufactured the laths from scrap wood, as opposed to other manufacturers who used prime wood and thus their company had a distinct price advantage and came to dominate the British market.

Folke had received his first letter from Olga, when she first arrived in New York. Her spirits appeared to be high, but they would change when she came to Jacksonville and discovered her mother's condition.

```
March 22, 1926
THE ROYAL HOTEL College Green in Bristol.

My own dearest Olga,
I was so glad to get your first letter from
America today when I arrived here this afternoon
from Liverpool via Birmingham. Your letter
has already been read several times and I am
very glad you had such a wonderful crossing. I
```

thought you were in bad all the time. Your letter started so sweet and I hope I get many more sweet letters from you. Write about everything, everything that concerns you, interests me Darling.

Just received a telegram from the office telling me all was all right and that the children are well.

I had to meet a business friend in Birmingham so had to stop over two trains and had time to sell him 5,000 bundles of laths.

Now here and I hope to be able to get to London by Wednesday, where there is a Timber Merchant dinner at the Savoy, to which I'm invited.

I do not like to make you tired with my usual but I did not sleep 10 minutes at a time all night. Either it is my dreadful longing for you or the long, long dreary Sunday I spent.

Long, long kisses in thousands and a big hug from you own longing Folke.

MARCH 26, 1926

Olga has arrived in Jacksonville and Folke is sad to find out about her mother's condition. He has a lot to report about his business trip.

March 26, 1926
HOTEL METROPOLE
London W.C.2
My Own Dearest Darling Olga,
It is now two days since I wrote you, but simply have not had the time, as the day before yesterday I left Bristol for London and immediately upon my arrival had to go the City to see four customer firms. Back to the hotel to change for the big dinner of The Timber Trades Federation, 400 people served in the ballroom at the Savoy, and a picture taken. You can trace me fine.

Yesterday from 10AM to 5.30PM in the city

again and back to the hotel to dress for dinner to join Alec and Ardly (?) at the Savoy, invited by them and then we danced up to at the Savoy, and she did not think I danced bad at all, rather the contrary.

This morning I went down to Victoria Station to see Peter Lexa and his three eldest children off for the reverie. After that I've been buying some small things for the children and tomorrow morning I sail home on "Patricia".

Anita is up and quite well (she had been ill at the convent school in Denmark) and I enclose the telegram which I asked her to send me to London.

Well Darling, your first letter from Jacksonville came this morning and I'm awfully sorry to hear that you found Mama so bad. I sincerely hope that it will not be long until I hear from you that she has got better. I quite agree with you, that she would do so much better to stay with us. Can't you persuade Mama to return with you but I suppose it is Willie who is in the way.

I will not any more repeat the longing and longing after you if it in any way hurts your stay, but please remember that you have many longing for you at home.

Regarding Bo-Erling, I cannot quite agree with you that it should have been better if he had gone with you, especially when your mother is sick and needs your attention constantly.

This will be the last letter from England and in going Eastwards it will be about one week interval between next letter.

I wished I was rich and could take an express steamer to you, because I do love you so much darling, I simply can't help it.

Now Darling, give my love to Mama and I'm sure that with all your energy you will soon get Mamma well, and I hope you both will return on the "Gripsholm" direct to Gothenburg.

I hope to find a lot of letters from you on my arrival in Gothenburg and that the North Sea will be smooth.

Love to all and at last my Darling, thousands of long, long kisses and a big hug from your own longing loving Folke

APRIL 1, 1926

Folke returns home from England to his children and more children arrive from their respective boarding schools. He really dotes on them. They will all have to spend Easter without their mother. This will be the second Easter without her. Last year Olga was in Brussels with her mother and her friend Joy Bratt. And now this.

Folke who already had written Olga a considerable number of letters from England, expected a lot of letters upon his return but was terribly disappointed not to find any at all. Olga explains in a letter why she has not written more:

"You must understand what a shock it was to me to find Mamma so ill. I was so distressed I could not write and I will never regret that I came. My presence has done Mama much good and she is now improving but I have been almost constantly with her with the exception of a few days during Easter down at Palm Beach. Please do not feel annoyed if you do not hear from me. I have more than you can ever imagine resting on my shoulders and will explain all when I return, this has been a most necessary trip and not much pleasure seeing my poor mother so very ill. Well Darling, forgive me and one day I will make up to you for my absence...

April 1, 1926
My own dearest Darling Olga,
I came home Monday after a smooth passage and found Billy, Bo-Erling, Gunilla and Ponkis in fine condition. They are so sweet. Tuesday, I and Billy went to Kungsbacka to get Anita, Mary,

Sonja and Sigrid by train (the girls had come home from the convent school in Denmark to spend Easter at home) and you can imagine how lovely they all are.

I feel awfully hurt, I have received one letter from New York and one from Jacksonville that's all, and have rushed to the office now for 6 days to try and see if any letters from you. None, and again none. The children's letter with the 20 kronor was posted March 16, my only letter from Jacksonville was posted on March 9, thus 7 days so far you have not given me a thought.

Can you be without writing me, I will do the same.

We are all at home now, only missing you dreadfully. Hjalmar and Ruth (Folke's sister) and Per-Axel (their son 13 years old) came ten minutes ago and will stay over Easter. Billy was in town with me yesterday and I bought him a coat, a whole suit, one pair extra trousers and a jumper. He looks nice now.

Have you got tired of all my longing?! I hope not. I feel very bad that you have not written me. The only pleasure you could give me.

Well Darling, a Merry Easter from us all and a long loving Easter kiss and a big hug from your own longing lonely Folke

PS
Since the mail takes about three weeks and you might already be on your way home, maybe there is no reason to bore you with any more of my epistles.

Love, Love, Love Darling Olga
From your own Folke

***

I cannot find any more letters from Folke, maybe he did get upset and did not write any more letters, or they were not saved, but his letter made Olga feel miserable and her answer:

"Folke your letter makes me miserable, I think of how you are feeling and of the great love you give me and I am away from you and must spend all the time alone but do me a favour and do not sit home alone but go out as much as possible and divert your mind and the time will soon pass and you will feel better..."

Folk expected Olga to come home during the month of April. Olga herself was vacillating, -- would her mother improve enough to go back with her, should she stay longer? Her mother had in the past, spent a lot of happy times in Sweden with Olga and Folke and their children. The children loved having their grandmother, Anita, around and my own mother, Gunilla, told me that the children would give their grandma drawings and perform songs for her and they would usually get a welcome coin from her. But now she was ill in Florida and Olga and Folke hoped they could bring her to Sweden and nurse her back to health. Olga tried to explain to Folke her dilemma:

"...All your very sweet letters received and I know you will be disappointed when I tell you it is impossible for me to make "Gripsholm". You cannot imagine what I have gone through, it is difficult to explain in a letter, but I'm trying hard to get Mama well and away from the dangerous clutches of many unscrupulous people around her, who would be only too glad if she died. I will try and leave on "Drottningholm" May 1st or "Stockholm" May 10th.

Mamma is better now but in great danger just now and she is unable to realize it. I want her to return with me, but how we can manage it, is guesswork, and you must be patient and soon all will be well. The heat is awful here...I am longing home and it is terrible for me, for you and the little ones and I feel I will never leave again.

... Dearest, you will understand, I am sure it is not easy for you, if only you had Anita with you (Anita, the eldest daughter, 16 at the time was at the convent in Denmark) *but the time will soon pass and I will never again leave you for so long a time. Try and not feel badly towards me for remaining longer than you wished but try and understand"*

Olga took a boat leaving May 8, from New York. She was not able to bring her mother with her. Sometimes it is good to know that history will not repeat itself, but five years later, in 1931, it did, and Olga went back in Jacksonville to look after her sick mother who again suffered a stroke.

On a more positive note, Olga writes that she has used her time there and has *"taken lessons on interior decorating and hope to use the garage or a little paint shop and go into business in the autumn"* and ends her letter that she is glad that Folke goes out more. She looks forward to coming home and hopes to remain there for some time and ends the letter *"Good night dearest Folke, I'm tired and this evening, a long kiss and hug from your devoted wife Olga"*

1931
THE GREAT DEPRESSION
AND A SICK MOTHER

In 1931, Olga was back in Jacksonville to visit her mother who had suffered another stroke. This time Olga brought her three daughters, Anita, twenty-one, Mary, eighteen, and Sonja, sixteen. She left her newborn baby Claes-Herbert behind as she had left her newborn Mary Carita behind eighteen years earlier. Then, in 1913, Olga and her two small children had been invited by her parents and they all had a lovely time going to the beach and motoring about. This time the circumstances were radically different.

Olga spent a great deal of time at the bedside of her mother who continually called for her. Her mother was largely immobile, could only move one arm and had trouble speaking, but she must have enjoyed seeing her grandchildren. Anita who this time was 21 years old, beautiful and clever, had a great time travelling and being adored by everyone she came in contact with.

The depression of 1929 was continuing and dominated the entire decade until 1939 when World War 2 ended it. Many of Olga and Folke's friends had suffered from the 1929 stockmarket crash and with the "Kreuger crash" of 1932, the situation was dire for a great number of people. In older age, Olga kept in contact with many such old friends who once had been more well-to-do but now lived on very small means.

Unlike them, Olga had not only a grand house, but also a most remarkable and devoted housekeeper, Linnea, who single-handedly kept the entire house going even by the time help were nearly unheard of in Sweden. Both Olga and Folke were loyal to their old friends and assisted as best they could. Olga and Folke both had kind and generous parents and they passed this generosity on to their own family and friends.

When Olga and her three daughters visited Jacksonville in 1931, it was against the backdrop of The Great Depression. Luckily, Olga's father had invested mainly in property and the family was spared. But many others were not that fortunate. All kinds of businesses suffered then, Folke and his father's usually very successful export business as well.

It was clear now that Olga's mother was at the end of her life. Olga wrote to Folke that anyone could get her mother to sign a cheque so she needed to be there, also she had to look after her own interests.

During an earlier visit, her two siblings had been given funds whereas she had not, which she had perceived as not quite fair. Folke encouraged her to look out for herself and to speak to Mr. W. Muhlback (the family lawyer?). Olga's mother no doubt realized that things must be settled and divided up, and a great deal of money must have been released as Olga was able to help Folke pay off his debts, no doubt a most welcome thing in the middle of a depression.

When Olga returned in June after a three months stay in Florida with her mother, not only had the financial matters been settled, her mother's condition had also been stabilized with the help of a new doctor. Olga felt that she could finally go home to her family and her little baby.

Four months later, her mother died. Poor Olga, how she must have wished she could have been with her mother at the end.

Olga's return to Jacksonville was certainly no pleasure trip. Folke wrote a letter nearly every day with news from their home, Lysholmen.

He remembered how hard it was for Olga in 1926, five years earlier, to spend over three months with her critically ill mother. At that time, in 1926, he probably did not realize the tremendous hardship it was for his wife during those months in Jacksonville. She had not written many letters then, devastated to see her mother so ill, but she told him in greater detail upon her return about the whole experience.

Folke, the ever understanding husband, was intent on doing what he could to be supportive. He wrote 53 letters (!) from March 5 to June 16. I have chosen to include two of them.

APRIL 13, 1931.

Folke had many expenses with a family of nine children, servants and a flat in town, plus the running of the large villa, Lysholmen. They also had two cars, a large Cadillac la Salle for Olga and a two seater Buick for Folke. The children went to private schools and Folke kept hunting dogs and bred grey partridges. Due to the depression, Folke's allowance did not cover all these expenses and he asked if Olga could help with the bills.

Folke had been out to play a game of golf and he mentions some prominent Gothenburg names playing that day.

As opposed to Folke's earlier letters, say, in 1909 and 1913, when Folke thought that the time passed slowly when Olga was gone, he did not have a chance feeling lonely now. He was surrounded with his children, and had Billy, Sigrid, Gunilla, Ponkis, Bo-Erling and the baby Clas-Herbert, to take care of. And one of them, Billy, was old enough to drive the family car. As noted earier, the three eldest daughters, Anita, Mary and Sonja were with Olga in Florida.

April 13, 1931
My Dearest darling Olga,
Well I was glad to get a letter from you this morning when I came to the office.

Saturday went out to Hovås and had a game with Gustav Lundberg and Putte Helling. There were quite a lot of people out. Gunnar Carlsson, Gunnar Engberg, Percy Lundberg, Wingstrand, Oscar Dickson, Percy Sinclair, James Dickson and several others. They all liked to see me out there.

Had dinner at 6PM and at 8PM. Billy (the oldest son age 19) drove the La Salle to Gothenburg with nurse Ida, Sigrid, Gunilla to get Bo-Erling and Ponkis who were at a birthday party at the Areschoughs. They all left me quite alone and I was looking after the baby who luckily slept the whole two and a half hours they all were in Gothenburg. Bo-Erling and Ponkis had enjoyed themselves very much.

Sunday at 10.30, Billy and I went to Hanhals to train the dogs. Fromell and Arvid Lignell came as well and for 2 hours we had a nice walk with the dogs and found 11 pairs of partridges and 16 hares.

As we arrived home, Filip Lindwall and wife came by for a visit and joined us for cocktails.

Mr. Lindwall liked our home so well and the baby was not at all afraid to get to her (Mrs. Lindwall).

Had dinner with the family, cold salmon with mayonnaise, chopped veal cutlets with spinach and fresh rhubarbs.

When Billy left at 7PM I went over to Lyons and played bridge with Erik and Sonja (Hertz) but finished at 11PM. I had luck all the time and won 9.80 kronor.

So a description of the children:

Billy looks a lot better now when he spends more time outdoors. He will get fresh air and exercise in June when he will begin his Military Service at Uddevalla. His superior will be a Captain Wockatz, married to Vera Kyhlberg.

Sigrid has got her second season ticket for the Särö-Gothenburg train and never seems to have any lessons. Her grades for Easter, not so good: Penmanship B-, Math B?, German C. Billy has promised to study with her, but her temperament is terrible. She more or less rules the entire house. I try flattery or jokes, but in vain. But then she can sometimes be so very sweet, well you know how she is.

Bo-Erling is well groomed and kind, but during Easter, his hair was untidy and he never came in time for the meals. He had done no mischief so I let him enjoy his freedom.

Gunilla, healthy and plump and fresh looking. She is kind but sometimes tries to copy Sigrid, but fails.

Ponkis, full of life spirit and respect for his elder brother (Billy) which is good sometimes.

The little baby (Claes-Herbert) is in my estimate doing very well and more sensible by the day. When he was brought into my room this morning for his slice of toast, he nearly said "Thanks". He looks like a peach. He walks much better and his legs have become almost straight. He only says Papa and Mama, but more words will surely come.

When we play chess he always comes and takes the pieces and says "chess" or "thanks" and moves them from square to square. He doesn't drool as much as he did when you were home, only when he gets sweets or something to eat. It is not necessary to take him to a doctor.

Yes my Dear, now you have heard what goes on at home, something I had wanted to do for a long time. Now you don't have to worry but enjoy your stay with your mother. I feel well, but my heart nerves are not always well, but I suppose it is because I long for you my Darling.

Come back when you consider that you have been there long with your folks and if you can make some arrangements to pay the bills, so much the better.

I kiss the children and send greetings to Una, Bob and all, love to Mama.

The longest and warmest kiss for you from your own
Folke.

MAY 11, 1931

Folke has every reason to rejoice, Olga was able to help with the debts and he could finally pay off a great number of bills. This is indeed fortunate, considering the world financial dilemma.

Folke is happy to be debt free and thanks Olga profusely and also tells her what he has bought for Sigrid's birthday.

Folke and the children brought a picnic and went to have a look at his hunting dogs kept in Fjärås.

Olga has been in Florida for some time with her three daughters and the eldest, Anita, has travelled a great deal in America. The question is raised whether she should stay on longer and remain after Olga returns to Sweden. Folke thinks not.

May 11, 1931
My own Dearest Darling Olga,
Well, the night before I leave on my round trip (business trip) I wish to give you all my heartiest thanks for the money you sent which arrived today at the bank. Olga Dearest, I cannot explain in writing how it felt today to settle my debts.

I'm sitting in Sigrid and Gunilla's room and Gunilla has got the measles very lightly, the temperature is only 38.8 and we put her to bed immediately last night.

The little baby is so cute and believe me, I'm really going to miss him a lot because he comes in my room every morning and in the sweetest voice he calls me Papa. I hear him already in (nurse) Ida's arms passing my door to be washed in the bathroom calling me Papa.

I have been to Sahlins (children's clothing store in Gothenburg) and bought Sigrid a red wool muslin dress for school (Kr. 19.50), she picked it out herself. Then to Gillblad and got a sweet little hat to match (kr. 18.50). She was very pleased with both.

Yesterday, Sunday, we all, Nurse Ida, the baby, Sigrid, (Gunilla had to stay at home), Bo-Erling, Ponkis, Billy and myself, all in the La Salle, Billy chauffeur, went to Fjärås to see how Hammar had arranged it and we brought a picknick. The dogs are allright, and only Zingo got "valpsjuka" (distemper). Hope the rest will not get it. Poor Zingo is much better but he had a hard attack of pneumonia.

Well Darling, I quite agree with Anita what she wrote me today, that there is not a mother or a wife, or a daughter to her Mama, like you.

Although I feel awfully lonesome I can understand you do not wish to leave your Mama. Come home when you feel like it Darling and when you have decided, please let me know so we all can have something to look forward to.

I do not wish to upset your plans with Anita,

but if you wish my opinion, I think she has been away long enough and could come home with you all (Olga, Mary and Sonja).

I spoke to Billy about boats and he said that if Anita likes his boat, she can buy it for Kr 200 and she can have it all to herself. If she does'nt like it, I will look for another one for her. If she likes it, I will have it painted and fixed up nicely and if she considers it a bit top heavy, we can fix it too.

Well, it's late now darling and Sigrid and Gunilla told to me, you must be "nuts" to write so much. Will have to stop.

Love to Mama, kisses to Anita, Mary, Sonja and to you my Dearest Darling, a long kiss and a big hug from your own, loving, longing and grateful Hubby

PS
You do not know how relieved and thankful I am. You have done a miraculous work and you must find some nice words for your Mama from me.
Kisses:

| x | x | x | x | x | x | x | x | x |
| x | x | x | x | x | x | x | x | x |

| x | x | x | x | x | x | x | x | x |
| x | x | x | x | x | x | x | x | x |

| x | x | x | x | x | x | x | x | x |
| x | x | x | x | x | x | x | x | x |

LETTERS FROM MÅÅTORP

During the Second World War (1939-1945), it was not safe for Olga to travel to America so there are no letters from Folke during this long period.

In 1946 many of Olga and Folke's children had got married and moved from home and Folke, who had spent many years improving Lysholmen, wanted a new project. He bought a small cottage farm near his hunting grounds in Fjärås, about an hour's car ride from their house by the sea at Särö -- no doubt for a very reasonable sum as it was in great need of repair and renovation.

By adding to and rebuilding the original cottage, he transformed it (taking a very active part in it himself) into a hunting lodge. The surrounding garden and forest were turned into a wild park. There were 6 hunting dogs, ducks, geese chickens and a large vegetable garden. In Spring, the entire garden and the well-kept forest exploded into an enormous expanse of bulbs and multi-coloured azalea and rhododendron bushes.

When you visited Olga and Folke, you were sure to be well taken care of. On a winter's day when you entered Määtorp, the hunting lodge, you were welcomed by a roaring fire, a raised corner fireplace which overlooked the rustic, open-beamed living and dining room -- and wonderful food to come.

There were many comfortable leather Chesterfield sofas, Windsor chairs and other dark stained furniture. You were guaranteed tremendous cooking from the superb cook Linnea. She also loved working in the garden and the forest, had embroidered sheets and towels with the name "Mååtorp" and had also made the oversized gingham napkins to accommodate my once thin, trim, and handsome grandfather's now large size. An old barn had been turned into a billiard room. The billiard table could be converted into a dining room for about thirty people, perfect for family gatherings or dinners for the hunting club.

Grandfather Folke loved his Mååtorp. All garden tools had been branded with "Mååtorp" and the benches in his park-like forest were numbered. This was important during hunting, and typical of organized Folke. He worked in the forest, clearing and cutting and had devised a special contraption where he and his helper made kindling wood packets so one could easily start a fire in the lodge's open fireplace. The kindling wood packets and ordinary fire wood, were stored in two large woodsheds faced with slender, debarked wood saplings -- charming and decorative. Using the same building method, he built a few open hunting cabins in the forest, where he and his fellow hunters could sit in comfort while waiting for animals to appear.

There was always something going on at Mååtorp, visitors and projects. Olga lived there off and on, spending time there between Lysholmen and going to Florida. By now four of her children had moved to Florida and their families were expanding.

Folke lived at Lysholmen, but he preferred his Mååtorp. Folke and Olga did not wish to leave

Lysholmen empty, so they rented it to various people at different times. Folke had to leave Mååtorp on many occasions to look after problems at Lysholmen and tired of that, he contemplated selling it, but Olga would not agree to it.

When Olga was in Florida, Folke wanted her to know everything that happened in his life at Mååtorp and Lysholmen. He had a charming enthusiasm, a keen interest in people and took a great pleasure in sharing his life and his observations with his dear Olga. The letters are sometimes extremely detailed so I have chosen certain passages:

DECEMBER 13, 1950

Linnea was very dear to everyone in the family and we always remembered her birthday on December 13. Olga had already left for Florida when Folke celebrated Linnea's 50th birthday so he was keen to tell her how Linnea's birthday was celebrated.

Anyone who knew Linnea, was well aware that Linnea never cared much for her exterior and did not like any personal attention. She refused to sit in a comfortable chair in the living room, and she never participated in any communal meals with the family unless it was something very special.

She mostly preferred to eat by herself and never any complete meal. There was not much anyone could do once she had decided how she wanted to do things. If anyone pushed too hard, her temper would flare quite violently.

But on this occasion, her 50th birthday, Linnea could not escape the celebration. Olga had sent a telegram, and Linnea would have coffee and cake with those who came to greet her on her birthday.

December 13, 1950
My beloved little "Mother",
Here I am again.
We at Mååtorp were happy to hear from you on Linnea's 50th birthday which we celebrated in the following way:

I had bought a torte and cookies and Linnea had baked one of her famous "vetekransar" (sweetbread wreaths). Linnea and I had coffee in the main living room and she was given the Cameo brooch and she was moved to tears. She also received a calf skin wallet with our money Kr 500 in new 10 kr notes and she appeared very happy.

After that, Carlsson (Folke's helper) arrived to dig the ditch up on the deer field and he received coffee and cake and the flag was hoisted.

At 12AM, Anita and (her children) Carita, Marion, Stella, Christel and their nanny arrived and we had coffee and sherry with them. The children got fruit, candy and a lot of sweets.

Anita had brought the ring for Linnea and it fit perfectly. Linnea also got some smaller gifts and Anita and Sven wanted to give her a fur coat(imitation) but it did not fit, so she was given 200 kronor instead which she gratefully put in her new wallet.

After that, Hjalmar arrived with a box of chocolates and flowers from Esther (his second wife after Ruth, Folke's sister). Linnea also received several money orders from friends...

...I better stop now because you will probably only read half of this uninteresting letter. I want to make sure that it gets posted before the 16th, the last day for air mail letters to arrive Florida before Christmas.

So one again my beloved Olga, have a Merry Christmas with the children and I send you a big hug and a long kiss,
Folke

DECEMBER 18, 1950
I have chosen this hunting story as being so typical of Folke and his life at Mååtorp with his society/ business/ hunting/ friends. He is a man of details eager to communicate. He has previously told Olga (not included below) what he and his hunting friends had to eat and then he wishes her to know about the hunt and a particular fox.

Later in the letter Folke mentions how daughter Gunilla and her husband, Tusse, (my parents) celebrated Lucia (a special Swedish celebration) on Saturday the 13th 1950. My mother was then 29 and my father 38. They had two children by this time. The reason this description is here because it is so typical of the kind of parties my parents and their friends had. They were never on a Friday because people worked Saturdays and there was always a great amount of liquor. The parties lasted until the early morning with "nattsexa" a breakfast type meal served between midnight and morning together with "snaps" (akvavit), then more liquor after that. Those kind of excesses are not common among young couples these days. Probably not that common...

```
December 18, 1950
My Darling Olga,
Of course I have got letters from you, one
written on the boat and mailed at Vinga, the
one posted December 5, in New York, also the
one dated December 12, and one today mailed
December 13...
   ....Saturday we started shooting here round
Mååtorp we heard the dogs barking down in the
woods of Lygnerud. I had placed all the other
10 guns round and about and had placed myself
just by the Rhododendrons near Mååtorp when a
fox appeared a few yards out of reach, right
```

through the "Linnea meadow".

My two shots had only the effect that the fox turned to the left and ran right through all the juniper bushes to bench No.7 where Philip (Krafft) was sitting with Carlsson (Folke's helper) and he shot it with his first shot, but not enough to kill him. Carlsson said to shoot another, but Philip said, "Do you think I will spoil the skin?"

Then the fox went right onto Ingo Busk, too near for a safe shot. So we really did not get that fox dead, but I'm quite sure that the fox will take no more chickens. What a pity, it was a very big fox.

Present at the shooting: Philip (Krafft), Sven (Hansson), Ingo (Busk), Lasse (Hedwall), Fritiof (Nordborg), Dan-Axel (Broström), Gustav-Adolf (Bratt), Per-Arne Wållgren, Claes Ekman, and Axel (Nordström).

While waiting for the weather report on the radio, Dan-Axel Broström (important shipping magnate) Philip Krafft and I sat before the fire and Dan-Axel who had never been here, asked to see the house and he thought it lovely. Then Gustav-Adolf Bratt and Dan-Axel Broström went back to Gothenburg and Philip and I joined the others down on the "Duvehed" fields where we shot eight hares, two of which had actually been shot at Määtorp earlier....

.....Tusse and Gunilla had a Lucia party for thirty-one people and they kept on until four in the morning and Tusse told me today, Monday, that they had continued partying on Sunday at Ingrid and Gunnar Tärby's to "phase down". So he was tired....

January 26th, 1951

Since Olga was in Florida over Christmas Folke feels responsible to keep her informed of the many

Christmas gifts he has given to the many family members and friends (the extensive list is not included below).

Folke is very interested in everything and asks Olga about the family property business in Jacksonville, Florida. "The Seminole Hotel" and "the Kress building", both of these companies had leases for 99 years from Olga's father William Dawson and there was some sort of negotiation going on at the time.

Olga was not home on her birthday and Folke tells her how they celebrated her birthday in a very special way:

Määtorp, Fjärås
January 26, 1951
Many thanks My Dearest Olga,
for your letter of January 20, telling me that you have troubles with your voting and must tell you that so far as I can remember you have not voted since you got that remark from Corcoran...)
...Now to your business regarding the estate. I would give you one advice not to sell any property now when you do not know what cash money is worth. Please let me know if there is any of the Seminole or the Kress lease expiring next year. I thought they were running for several more years, but I remember you told me some time ago that Kress had offered a higher amount to get their lease renewed as they were planning to build a higher building on the property, or rather to get the lease to run for a longer period than contracted for. Please let me know if anything of interest in this matter arises but I suppose you have good advice from Charlie (lawyer son-in-law in Jacksonville.)...

Olga Dear, on Monday January 10th, was your 60th birthday, Linnea had baked two large "vetekransar" sweetbread wreaths and donuts and ginger snaps and Linnea, Carlsson and I went to the Old People's home in Fjärås with all this and coffee. The matron there was very grateful for this....

DECEMBER 27, 1955

Folke and Linnea were quite isolated in Mååtorp, deep in the forest, the steep road was hard to navigate at the best of times and occasionally impossible in winter. They were often snowed in for days.

Today with 4-wheel-drive cars, we can easily manage difficult hills in winter conditions, but such cars were not available in those days. Folke had a Cadillac that weighed 2 tons, but it still had rear wheel drive and could easily get stuck or slide on ice or snow.

As usual, Folke's descriptions are detailed and vivid. Here he tells Olga about his Christmas adventure with snow ice and rain.

December 27, 1955
Mååtorp, Fjärås
My Dearest Olga,

This is the third day after Christmas and before I drive into Kungsbacka I will tell you how I spent Christmas.

The night between Friday and Saturday, we had another hard wind and heaps of snow and I was again blocked at Mååtorp. Promises all day to have the road down to the main road plowed before 1PM but by 5.50PM it was temporarily unblocked. Carl-Eric (the local taxi driver and much used by Folke) tried to come up here immediately but it took him an hour. First he had to reverse for a bus and got stuck in a ditch.

Well it took him half an hour to come up my hill. Then we tried the main road to the Fjärås church, but there were 4 cars stopped on the icy road. He backed all the way to the milk table, went to the left via Myra to get two Moccha Tortes (a specialty from the local bakery) that Linnea had ordered for Anita and Gunilla.

We came to Gustav Andersson on pure ice in pouring rain and the car went from one side to the other and Mr. Andersson advised us that if we wanted to keep alive, to turn back to Määtorp. Do that and don't risk your lives.

We did it all right and both Linnea and I thanked God that we made it home. So I had lutfisk and cheese alone. On Christmas Day, also alone, it rained all day and it removed most of the snow on the roads...

MARCH 19, 1956

Life for Folke at Määtorp was pleasant, but he had Lysholmen, rented or not, to look after as well. The water source for the house was situated a considerable way from the house and a pump-house by the main road sent water in a pipe over a large meadow, up through rock to Lysholmen. Much could and did go wrong with the pump and the water pipes and Folke had a lot of trouble trying to solve the problems that arose, either a frozen pump or water that did not go up to the second floor etc.. The furnace including the burner and circulation pump gave Folke trouble too. (After Folke died, it was Linnea who dealt with all these matters). Folke informed Olga about all, and always in great detail, but in this letter, he was happy to give a particularly detailed and pleasant account of a different nature, namely of *Victor Hasselblad's 50th birthday*. Folke knew that Olga wanted to know all the details of their friend, the famous inventor of the Hasselblad Camera -- and his big birthday party.

Mååtorp Fjärås, March 19, 1956
My Dearest Olga,
Well, here you have me again and I hope this will reach you before you leave Jacksonville. First I will wish you very welcome home and hope you will have a very good journey.

Vicke's (Victor Hasselblad) 50th birthday was celebrated first with a reception at Råö (a large estate on the coast). There was a reception and lunch for everybody who came, about 150 people. A big lunch (buffet style) was served with snaps (akvavit) and beer, coffee etc. I only drank a glass of beer as I had to drive my car.

Flowers, flowers en masse. I have never seen anything like it, presents, expensive in china, glass and silver etc. I was only there an hour and they were so pleased to see me there.

For dinner, at Östra Hamngatan 3 in Gothenburg, in the same flat that Vicke was born, they served cocktails, snaps, (akvavit) with caviar, ? sandwiches in the room where where they have their hats (?) exhibited, but that day, there was one from every year, fifty years back.

After that we moved up in elevators, twenty at a time in their baggage lifts to one of their big luncheon places. A hundred people for dinner in full dress suit. I looked very nice in all my decorations.

Professor Tiselius, Nobel Prize winner, had Erna (Mrs. Hasselblad) to dinner and on her other side, I was there with Vicke's sister, remarried a Captain Dyrsen on her other side.

Vicke had Vera to his right and this on account that Vera was only one day older than Vicke. Marianne Bratt and Ulla Broström were there without husbands who were in Stockholm on business meetings. Philip and Tyra (Krafft?), Dagmar and Herbert Ewert, Ulla Kruger, Mrs Professor Olof Rydbeck, Gerda Kjellberg and a load more were there.

Soup, sole, duck mousse and ice cream served on ice cameras, copies of the Hasselbald camera.

Ingolf Schander was there, Göran von Essen, Yngve Beckmans (?). I handed over the engraved silver flask from the hunting association and from me, one of those little hunting chairs and a pair of hunting gloves.

Vicke wrote today:

"Dear Folke, thank you for coming and gilding my existence on the 8th of March. It was very dear to Erna and me to have you. And thank you for the fine hunting chair which I have just "baptized". It is quite splendid and thank you also for the most useful hunting gloves. And also thank you for handing over the most cherished hunting club, silver flask (engraved with all their names) which I hereby thank you Mr. President for. Your fine speech during dinner we remember with great fondness.

My warmest thank you for everything, affectionately Vicke"

JANUARY 31, 1960

Folke produced a considerable number of letters from Måätorp and there are only glimpses of them in this book. His love for detail and his caring for people and animals is touching. He had an eagerness to describe and communicate and these lines in this letter are very special.

The 60 year old Linnea and the 74 year old Folke had watched a Lassie film (the famous Collie dog) together on the black and white TV at Måätorp. Linnea cried and Folke almost cried too, he admitted. And of course Olga had to be brought in on this experience too. I am amazed how the man could muster the enthusiasm and energy to retell this story and to remember all the details so clearly. You certainly were a special one, grandpa Folke!

Måätorp Fjärås, Sunday January 31, 1960
My Dearest Olga
Many thanks for your Thursday letter, but my

Dear why did you write such a long letter when you should rest your eyes...

...Yesterday we, I mean Linnea and I, looked at TV and I must say that a Lassie film has never been so good. Linnea cried with tears and almost I as well.

Lassie was examined by their house doctor who told the family that Lassie would be blind within thirty days as nothing could be done.

The next night, the boy left and instead of going to school, he went to the nearest city hospital to try to get an operation. He was sent away from the hospital and told that no dogs were allowed. The boy found out who was the best doctor in the department, a Dr. Masar, and he tried to get him at his private clinic but was told by the nurses to leave, the doctor did not have time to see him they said.

However, he found out the doctor's room number and walked into same and found him sitting at the desk, walked up with Lassie. The doctor asked him what he wanted. "Please operate on my dog, she is so good and I was told that you are the only one who can do it. Please doctor, I know you have made many operations by putting a live nerve eye (transplanted?) and I'm willing to give one of mine."

The doctor was touched and looked at Lassie's eyes and said that there was a very small chance for a successful operation. The boy held up a bag and said that all he had was three dollars and ten cents and that the doctor could have that. The doctor cancelled all the scheduled patients and after thirty days he took off the bandages from Lassie and placed the boy, mother and grandpa against the wall in the room. He told Lassie to go to the boy. At first Lassie could not see so well but then Lassie began to bark and ran to the boy.

Excuse my long story, but the dog played so well...

1961
FOLKE'S LAST LETTERS

JANUARY 12, 1961
Olga had departed for New York two days earlier, on her birthday January 10, on the Swedish passenger liner "Kungsholm". Her trip to Florida that year was ill-omened from the very beginning and little did she know that she would soon have to return to Sweden. On the way over she experienced hurricane weather and arrived to a freezing and snowed in New York. The train to Florida had to be thawed out many times and she arrived late to Jacksonville, also under a severe cold-spell. Olga wrote that Florida felt much colder than Sweden as the houses were not well insulated.

The economic climate in America was equally chilly. Olga's three sons who were in the building business together, had been hit by the mini-depression. Olga wrote later to Folke that it was just as well that he did not come on this trip with her -- "everyone was broke" and they would not have been able to entertain as they previously had. Her daughter's family and her sister seemed to be the only financially stable just then.

Mååtorp Fjärås
January 12, 1961
My Dearest Olga,
Many thanks for your telephone call the same day you left, the 10th, and also for your call from North of Scotland. I heard your voice very clearly in the beginning, but another call came in.

However I was happy that you had such nice weather and I hope it will continue. You must have have had fun celebrating your 70th birthday two years in succession.

Yesterday we had a sunny day but last night we had 12 degrees Celcius below zero, it is a little milder now at 7AM. I am really missing you very much and have difficult to get to sleep before three at night.

(I have omitted his description of all his considerable shopping trips and errands in Kungsbacka, the closest town).

Have spoken with all the children about your call from "Kungsholm". Linnea looks after me and the first night she did not go to bed until three, because she was worried about me snoring. The bell into her room is working OK. I have brought a fresh battery.

(I have omitted a lengthy description of the problem with the heating system at Lysholmen which at the time was rented to a family Ohlson. It finally got solved after the oil tank and burner were cleaned and a lot of energy had been spent by many people).

I miss you so much, but troubles like the above kill time. Hope you have had a good journey and are feeling well. All my love to you all in Jacksonville and kiss them all and take your share with a hug and kiss
   from your Folke.
   Linnea sends her love.

January 21, 1961

Before Olga left, she had set aside a lot of items, gifts, furniture, her decorated Swedish Folk Art items, Linnea's home made candy etc. They had to be packed and sent on to Jacksonville on a separate cargo vessel, "Maltesholm". When Olga had left ten days earlier on a regular passenger vessel she was only able to bring ordinary luggage.

When she sometimes travelled to Florida on a cargo vessel that went from port to port, say from Gothenburg to Jacksonville, a lengthy journey via a lot of other ports, she could load her cabin full of gifts, furniture, painted items. There were usually 3-4 cabins for passengers on these cargo ships. It was a convenient way of bringing things direct from Gothenburg to Jacksonville and vice versa. To everyone's delight.

A cargo ship stopped in many ports on the way and Olga, would get off in the various ports and buy old things that she would paint and decorate in her cabin -- she had her painting gear with her and wasn't going to waste any time.

An author, Greta Molander wrote an amusing description of the charming and eccentric "Olga" whom she met on a freighter. She also made a humorous drawing of Olga arriving at the freighter with a porter and cart load of antique pots and pans and various gadgets that Olga consequently worked on in the cabin and then, on arrival in Jacksonville, distributed to all her children and grandchildren.

At Määtorp, Linnea and Folke had been busy packing all the items destined for Florida -- four very large parcels. The local taxi-driver "Karl-Erik" who frequently drove Folke and Olga to various places, used a trailer to haul these items into Gothenburg and the forwarding company Jonsson, Sternhagen & Co., Folke's old company, where his son Billy would see to all the paper work and make sure that the four parcels were safely loaded onto the freight vessel "Maltesholm".

January 21, 1961
Mååtorp, Fjärås, Saturday
My Dearest Olga,
How happy I was when your telegram was delivered by phone yesterday morning that you were safe in New York. I know from two calls with Nordenborg that Sunday and Monday, the ship did not make more than 10 knots and better the following day with 15 knots. I suppose you got a touch of the hurricane which sunk the Texas Tower No 4 outside new York.

Since my last letter, nothing special happened. Jan and Peder (two grandchildren) stayed from 3PM to 10.30PM after TV, nearly nine hours. They were very pleased.

One thing after the other happened with the heating at Lysholmen but now it works all right, the main reason was that the tank had never been cleaned since we installed it about fifteen years ago.

Thursday, Karl-Erik taxi took your four parcels from here to Billy's yard in Gothenburg. Johansson went along to show the way. Just spoke to Billy. Everything went fine and "Maltesholm" leaves today.

Linnea is doing her usual work, cleaning, washing and giving me dieting food, and I feel better altogether. On the 16th, I got the rent for Lysholmen, for three months.

I hope Folke Jr. (Ponkis) does not come to get you in his car in New York as I gather from reports that snow in large quantities kept Kennedy from coming to Washington for his installment as President yesterday.

Kisses and hugs my Darling
and hug the Jonsson clan.

January 30, 1961
It is amazing what an interest Folke takes in everything that goes on in the world

January 30, 1961
My Dearest Olga,
Well, how pleased I was when I received your letter from Jacksonville. I had followed your trip to New York and gathering from TV, radio and newspapers, you must have had quite a bad time coming to Jacksonville.

I had started a letter yesterday but had, sorry to say, scolded you a little bit not to have sent two words by cable that you had really arrived in Jacksonville -- never mind.

You should be here instead of in chilly Florida. It is +5 C and the buds on the birch trees look like they do in spring. The bulbs outside the kitchen terrace are about 1-2 inches above ground and Linnea told me that the snow drops have started to come up.

Linnea takes good care of me and both cats are coming in my bed every day. I hear the radio and see the TV.

I suppose you have read in the U.S.A papers about Santa Maria, a Portuguese passenger steamer with 600 passengers and over 300 sailers being captured by robbers and the Santa Maria is now hunted all over round about Tenerife and the captain (the pirate) has said that he will rather sink the boat than be caught.

I hope you have a wonderful time with the family. Take good care of yourself. In the next letter, tell me how you feel. I am better but far from strong enough to work as usual...

February 14, 1961
Folke has a visit from his nephew Sven Hanson, a fellow hunter and a dear friend who spent many weekends with his best friend Folke.

Folke tells an interesting story about two hunting dogs that were saved because of him. He seemed very pleased to relate how he saved them from being shot.

February 14, 1961
Mååtorp, Fjärås
My dearest Olga,
I thank you for both your letters, the one you started and Sigrid (their daughter in Jacksonville) finished. Also your newsy letter from the Greenfield Plantation and was happy to hear that all of them are well down on the farm.

Depression generally always come with the change of presidents until the new government can stabilize the different markets and now the terrible state of Congo will no doubt have only troubles and no one knows what is going to happen. I wish you were safely here back again. Florida is so near the Cuba (the Cuban missile Crisis happened the following year in October).

I am gradually getting better and reducing to nothing all the different medicines I have tried. One main thing for me is to eat half of what I have been used to and certainly hope it is not a temporary gain of health.

Since my last letter, only Sven (Folke's nephew and close friend) came on Friday after shooting hare on Rörö (an island outside Gothenburg). I was not there and Sven stayed here until Sunday afternoon. He and Johansson (caretaker) shot a hare each.

Sven and Johansson discussed quite a lot about Loola and Boy, you know the Beagles (two of the six hunting dogs Sven and Folke owned together). Sven certainly pleaded to get rid of them, the dogs being being worthless for shooting.

On Monday, when Sven had left, Johansson and I took them down in the woods where we were working without guns, and we let them go where they wanted and after 10 minutes they found "deer" and believe me, we have never had such splendid dogs driving first one big buck for at least two hours and perfect barking. Then Loola came home, but after that Boy must have got another and did not come home until 11PM.

I think the main reason is that the dogs are scared of the guns which is not so difficult to treat them for.

Love to you all and take care of yourself.
A big kiss and hug, Your
Folke

FEBRUARY 28, 1961
FOLKE'S LAST LETTER TO OLGA

Folke seemed to be feeling better and he was well enough to work clearing brush in the forest. He always had a brandy flask with him in case he had trouble breathing. As usual, he had many visitors.

Until the very end Folke kept "talking" to Olga in his letters and it is remarkable that he kept such youthful enthusiasm and interest in life. When other men might have lost their spirit, he had the energy and enthusiasm to express what he felt and had experienced. The letters to his beloved Olga, until the very end, were dated, and numbered, still in his fine penmanship.

His last letter is addressed to Olga c/o their daughter Sigrid on Ortega Terrace in Jacksonville. Folke wrote that he would mail this letter the following day, but the envelope, bears no postmark.

When Folke finished his letter he wrote his last words, ever, to Olga: *"I am somewhat better, but my neck is getting stiff again, I wish you were here"*. Folke probably had his first stroke that very night. Two weeks later he was dead.

Folke was taken to the Varberg hospital and it was said by some family members that he died because he was not allowed his brandy flask, his constant companion and saviour in many breathless moments. But I have been told that his son Billy smuggled brandy to him so that theory is probably not correct, a first stroke is usually followed by further strokes and Folke died two weeks later, before Olga arrived home.

The envelope containing letter number ten, Folke's last letter to Olga -- full of Folke's typical sweetness and devotion for his wife Olga -- lay on the table waiting for Olga on her return to Mååtorp from Jacksonville Florida.

February 28, 1961
Mååtorp, Fjärås
My Dearest Olga,
Since my last letter, nothing special has happened of great importance except the pleasure of hearing from you, that you painted some pictures at the farm and that Florida's warm climate had started.

Here it is still warm weather and bunches of snow drops are in full bloom, even daffodils are budding outside the kitchen terrace. The pigeons have come and are cooing something tremendous. The thrush that usually makes a nest behind your atelje' (painting workshop) has already had babies. I only hope that we do not get too strong a freeze in March/April, but there is no ice anywhere on the West coast and the ships will soon start trafficking lake Vänern. In Skåne the farms have already started their spring activities.

The children and grandchildren are all, always welcome to come, Kenneth just returned from a ski vacation in Austria and he is very tanned after fourteen days there. During the school holidays Billy's twins went to Denmark, Marion has been skiing and the Södergren children have been to Norway, but I feel better and work in the forest instead of going to the Skogsborg sanatorium, it would cost too much.

I have not had to ring for Linnea at night until the night between Sunday and Monday, when I woke up from some strange sound in the heating system and there was no heat. We went down to the furnace room, I brought my brandy flask, and we discovered that there was no water in the furnace and together we filled it, but it would not start. At 8 AM I called for Johansson and there was soot in the burner and when that got fixed, it all worked fine again.

There was an "invasion" of visitors here at Määtorp last Sunday. Erik Lund and Bibbi came at 1PM and we had coffee, sandwiches and torte and they left at 2.30PM.

I met Sven and Camilla by the cars and we took a walk around the grounds. After they left, we met Billy and Bengt-Folke and we continued drinking coffee until they left.

Anita and Sven are busy having business dinners with Japanese guests and agents and they will have baptism for Carita's baby, I think she will be called Anita, Maria Therese, not quite sure. I enclose the recipe you asked me to send.

Anita is coming to Fjärås Friday morning to pick up some mocha tortes (a speciality at a local bakery).

The realtor Kleborg rang on Saturday and asked if we are willing to sell Lysholmen for 550,000 Swedish crowns. I told him that my wife was not interested. I told him jokingly that if the price were 800,000, then my wife might be interested to let go of her beloved Lysholmen.

Love to all the families, also from Linnea. I will mail the letter tomorrow. Kiss and hug, your
Folke.

I am somewhat better, but my neck is getting stiff again, I wish you were here...

OLGA AND FOLKE

My grandmother Olga died at 89, having survived Folke by eighteen years. She spent two weeks at a private hospital in Gothenburg more or less fading away.

She was very restless toward the end and we sensed that she had something on her mind, something she regretted or wished she had done differently.

She had borne nine children and had many grandchildren and great-grandchildren who now resided on two continents. Her life had been eventful, full of many choices. Of course there would always be regrets, but if I am to speculate that grandmother Olga at the end of her long life had any regrets, I would imagine that they would have concerned her husband Folke.

She had left him alone in Sweden on many occasions when she went on her extensive trips to Florida. Loving and devoted Folke was always there when she came back. She could always count on Folke -- he was her constant. In 1961, when she left for Florida, she naturally expected her dear Folke to be there, alive and well when she returned later in the year. As he always had been. She was simply not prepared for anything else.

I know that grandmother Olga felt very guilty for having been away when my grandfather died in 1961. He had pleaded with her not to go, no doubt as he had pleaded many times before when she left him for Florida. But there was nothing that could have predicted that Folke would not live through what he was eagerly looking forward to: celebrating his 75th birthday in May.

Folke, the happy loving spirit in Olga's life was gone and she was ill prepared. She was inconsolable and her daughters Anita and Gunilla who subsequently stayed with her for many months at Mååtorp, Folke's beloved hunting lodge, were concerned for their mother and the many hours she spent alone with the dead Folke in the "chapel", a converted white washed garage. Folke lay there embalmed for many weeks until he could be buried in a specially prepared concrete chamber. It took a long time to construct the underground concrete chamber where Folke's body would eventually be placed in a sealed zinc coffin, all according to his wishes.

Folke was a kind soul and explicitly and profusely expressed his love for Olga. Not many wives, I suspect, will ever have such a sweet natured husband. His many letters are ample proof. But was she as demonstrative as he was? Was she as "good" as *he* was?

Olga had plenty of time to reflect on this as she sat with Folke in the chapel day in and day out for all those weeks. Did she bring his letters to read? What did she say to him that she had not been able to say to him when he was alive? In comparison to his gentle personality and generosity of spirit, she might have felt that she could have been a better wife to Folke.

But she was the woman she was. She was the Olga, Folke once fell madly in love with and couldn't be without. And he was the man he was, the Folke, her "baby", that Olga once fell madly in love with.

A feeling of guilt is fruitless, but a phenomenon that we often indulge in when in despair and choked by loss, we try to navigate in a severely altered landscape.

Olga decided that Folke's grave stone should have the following inscription:

"Folke Jonsson 1864 -1961 Loved by everyone"

To those who never met Folke, the words sound very endearing, but one must have known Folke in person to truly understand why those words were chosen for him. He really was a man liked and loved by everyone. There was not an ounce of malice in him and he cared enormously for his family and friends. Reading his letters might also help to understand why Olga chose those words.

Folke's nephew, Per-Axel Atterbom, the talented son of Folke's beloved sister, Ruth, who knew his uncle Folke intimately, wrote these fine and illuminating lines in the Svenska Dagbladet newspaper on March 24, 1961 (translated from the Swedish)

FOLKE JONSSON IN MEMORIAM.

There are people who in their lives appear to realize a synthesis between heaven and earth. They are bound to the one, but give the appearance of the other. Folke Jonsson was one of the chosen ones. Life was lavishly generous, but also generous through him to others. He lived life on earth with great intensity and with great happiness because of what had been given to him. But he also gave to others with the same lavish generosity he had enjoyed. He valued each person equally as much. Whoever he encountered, he made them part of what he enjoyed. He was a good trusted friend. His heart and home were open to all. His word was as firm as his handshake. He could never speak ill of anyone. That was simply not in his nature.

His lust for life covered everything and everyone. Whatever he was involved in, he managed well. He prided himself in making the best of whatever he was involved in. He always expressed the same stormy lust for life and an intensive consideration for others whether he dealt with the future of his children, the comfort of his friends, any chore, an evening with friends and family, a hunt or starting a new garden project.

He was indeed one of the chosen ones who until the very end retained a boyish and a youthful enthusiasm. As the saying goes, those whom the gods love, die young. Folke left the big feast of life while he still enjoyed it. He left it with the uncorrupted, courageous and trusting spirit of a young man.

His memory will live on -- energizing and strengthening us all.
Peace be with him.

P.A Atterbom
Särö March 23, 1961

FAMILY FACTS

OLGA MIMS (DAWSON) JONSSON 1890/91 - 1978
FOLKE JONSSON 1886 - 1961

THEIR CHILDREN:
Anita 1910
Billy 1911
Mary 1913
Sonja 1915
Sigrid 1917
Bo-Erling 1918
Gunilla 1921
Ponkis (Folke) 1922
Claes-Herbert 1930

OLGA'S PARENTS:
Anita (Ball) Dawson 1858 - 1931
William Dawson 1856 - 1916

FOLKE'S PARENTS:
Ragnhild (Lundgren) Jonsson 1864 - 1903
Axel Jonsson 1844-1931

THE AUTHOR

Leif Södergren is the grandson of Folke and Olga Jonsson. He grew up in and now lives in Gothenburg, Sweden.

He has a B.A. and Master of Arts Degree in American Studies at California State University, San Diego.

He has worked with International Marine Insurance for many years.

He now works with publishing, writing, and has had one Swedish and one English blog since 2009.

Like his grandmother Olga, he also paints Swedish Folk Art.

www.ingramcontent.com/pod-product-compliance
Lightning Source LLC
Chambersburg PA
CBHW051751040426
42446CB00007B/313